Fearless & Persuasive SPEAKING

A Communication Guide for Leaders

Ken Bradford

Pierce Publishers
Dallas, Texas

Published by:
Pierce Publishers
P.O. Box 794002
Dallas, TX 75379-4002
972-233-9484
www.leaderscourse.com

LCCN: 00-131074
ISBN: 0-9679708-1-4
PRINTED IN THE UNITED STATES OF AMERICA

Cover design: Peri Poloni, www.knockoutbooks.com
Interior design: indypub, LLC, www.indypub.com

Publisher's Cataloging-in-Publication
(Provided by Quality Books, Inc.)

Bradford, Ken.
    Fearless and persuasive speaking : a communication guide
for leaders / Ken Bradford. -- 1st ed.
    p. cm.
    ISBN: 0-9679708-1-4
    LCCN: 00 131074

    1. Public speaking. 2. Interpersonal communication. I.
Title.

PN4121.B73 2002   80.51
                                         QBI00-35

Dedicated to those who strive to make a difference.

We know what we are, but know not what we may be.
—William Shakespeare

CONTENTS

Contents

Contents

INTRODUCTION

What if every time you stood up to speak to a group you could be yourself — at your best? What if you could be articulate, funny, charismatic, and persuasive...whenever you chose...no matter how big your audience was?

The potential is there, if you choose to tap it. You're already a successful, motivated, intelligent adult. Whether it's in the office or at home, you know how to communicate your message to get the job done. Every day you solve problems, achieve goals, and build and deepen relationships with people from all walks of life.

So why is it that the idea of speaking before a group puts you into a tailspin, bringing on sweaty palms, an urge to flee, and a rising sense of panic you haven't felt since adolescence? Why is it that you can be expressive and animated one-on-one or in small groups, full of enthusiasm, wit and charm, but you turn into an emotionless robot the minute you're asked to stand up before an audience?

One thing is certain: if you feel this way, you are not alone. It may seem like everyone else takes public speaking in stride, talking to a group of 60 as effortlessly as they check their e-mail every morning, but research proves you've got a lot of company out there. In fact, according to many surveys, more people in the United States are afraid of public speaking than of dying!

Maybe you're not even looking for recognition or a stage upon which to perform. You may be getting dragged kicking and screaming into the spotlight. Perhaps you've reached the stage in your career or your life, where the need to make a speech has come up because of a work or personal commitment. But think about it: if you've been asked to speak or present your ideas, it's because other people have recognized that you have something valuable to say. You're someone who's worth listening to because of your common sense, background, life experience, training, education, or a combination of all of these factors.

As a speaker, you are by definition already a leader. As a leader, you must be able to organize and communicate your ideas in a way that will move your audience toward an end.

But how do you get out of your own way to give your best performance? How do you stop mentally judging yourself while you're at the podium? How do you avoid feeling as self-conscious as the skinny kid getting picked last for basketball? How do you overcome a fear that can range from simple butterflies to sheer, heart-pounding terror, depending on the situation?

That's what this book is all about. If speaking were just a matter of standing up, opening your mouth, and waiting to see what came out, there would be no need for another book. This book is your personal road map to becoming a fearless and persuasive speaker.

So how do you begin? You begin by realizing that fearless and persuasive speaking is not brain surgery. It's simply an applied science that requires planning, organization, commitment, and action: skills you have already mastered in other areas of your life. The ability to lead groups is not genetic or something you are "born with." It is a skill that can be learned. Mastering it is simply the next natural progression in your track record of success.

Fearless and Persuasive Speaking

I wrote this book to help people speak fearlessly and persuasively in front of groups, but also to fill a real need in the business world. To the best of my knowledge, no other public speaking book addresses the public speaking issues many adults wrestle with today:

- You are not the only person who occasionally feels overwhelmed trying to "get it together" while facing the possibility of public humiliation.
- There is no such thing as a born speaker anymore than there are born leaders, born managers or born garbage collectors.
- Most of our public speaking role models have failed us. Mentors are few and far between.
- There are hundreds of rules for the mechanics of speaking, but little coaching on how to be yourself, your best, natural self while speaking.
- Traditional educational systems have emphasized knowledge and content while neglecting delivery. But content without effective delivery will rarely compel and hold interest, or persuade.
- Conversely, voters elect candidates with the strongest delivery skills. (Consider the last five presidential elections.)

It's clear that today's business leaders need more than knowledge to be successful. Many a career rises and falls on the ability or inability of an employee to state an idea or a set of facts clearly and concisely, according to writer William Zinsser.

Leaders need to be able to translate their knowledge into a concise vision and persuade a group to take action, whether that group numbers five or five hundred. After all, persuasion is a critical business skill across all levels of management, whether you're speaking to a board of directors, presenting a proposal to prospective customers, or explaining a new policy to employees. And you need the ability to easily tap into that skill no matter what size group you're facing. You never know when an appointment with one person will suddenly become an opportunity to speak to a committee of eight or even ten decision-makers!

In the modern information age, no one person has all the answers. Speaking has become a participative exercise rather than a lecture format. As Thomas McGaffey says in his book *The Courage to Lead,* leadership happens in conversations — conversations that produce action, paint a vision, inspire, build trust, solve problems and strengthen relationships. But most people manage conversations best in private. They could significantly improve their productivity and efficiency if they had equal skill in public forums; but unfortunately most executives are better trained to manage people and data than to manage themselves in front of groups.

Before the World Trade Center tragedy, George W. Bush spoke mostly from notes and sounded stilted and rehearsed. In the days after the September 11 tragedy, he found his voice. You may never face such a difficult situation, but you may well find yourself trying to find your voice under pressure, too.

Fearless and Persuasive Speaking suggests methods for owning your message, not borrowing it. Far too many leaders believe that politically-fashioned words, written by someone else, will make a better impression than their own thoughts and beliefs. But passion, insight and conviction don't come from a speechwriter, subordinate, or department head. The conviction of your words, powered by the lessons life has taught you, will influence others far more than anyone else's words coming from your mouth.

John F. Kennedy wrote the powerful speech that he gave to the citizens of Berlin, who were so stirred by his words that they almost rioted. Lincoln penned the immortal Gettysburg Address on the back of his lunch sack while he rode the train from Washington. Both men took the time to capture the right words for what they needed to say at a crucial moment, and then said it — without fear and with great persuasion.

Fearless and Persuasive Speaking

The Japanese word for teacher is *sensei*, which means honored leader. In addition to learning to inspire, motivate, and lead when you speak, you'll receive an extra dividend in this book. You'll learn to honor and respect your ideas…to unleash the power of your unique message … and to have fun exploring your newfound capacity to move others. Armed with the techniques in this book, you'll spend more time formulating your message and less arranging the order of your slides. Your presentations will persuade and not merely inform.

What have I discovered that educators and institutions have been missing? That speaking is mostly an emotional skill, and that fear must be overcome before persuasive skills can be developed. By following the practical truths in this book — designed to be readily applied — you will be more confident of what you have to say as well as more certain of the outcome you'll achieve after you've said it. In *Fearless and Persuasive Speaking*, what you learn about good public speaking will seem like something you've known all along: it is basically a purposeful conversation with individuals who happen to be a group.

In the last 20 years, I have listened to an average of 44 speeches a week from people of diverse backgrounds and education. What I have found in two decades of classroom and private instruction is that students of public speaking need far more encouragement than correction. During my career, and in the personal development course I've been teaching since 1992, I have given that encouragement by helping students to grow — to build on natural abilities that have been neglected or misused. I've seen people grow in many ways: the very shy become more confident; the abrasive become more personable. I have distilled both lessons and errors into the 23 chapters that follow. May they guide and inspire you.

–Ken Bradford

A school should not be a preparation for life.
A school should be life. – Elbert Hubbard

ONE

FEAR

You are not alone. Fear affects everyone.

R oy's voice over the phone sounded frustrated, almost angry. "Can you come over this evening and talk to my wife about public speaking classes?" he asked.

Roy had been the first person to respond to an advertisement that I had placed in a local business journal announcing a new public speaking class. Excitedly, I told him yes. Two hours later, I knocked on the door of his home.

"There she is!" He pointed to his wife Diane, slumped dejectedly on an ottoman in the family room. I asked Roy if Diane and I could speak alone. He agreed, lit a cigar and walked down the hall, pulling a door shut behind him.

Clearly relieved that Roy was gone, Diane began speaking in a soft, halting voice: "I have to start speaking to groups and I don't want to do it."

"What's the situation?" I asked. "My church has made me an elder, their first female elder. I am in charge of the youth group, and now every month I'm supposed to speak to the board. And I'm terrified. I don't know what I am going to do."

She explained her dilemma. Over the past three years, Diane had created such an excellent youth program that the elders had recognized her vision and wanted her on the board. Now, she was so scared that she was entertaining serious thoughts of quitting the program as well as the church.

"Diane," I said. "You really love the work you are doing with the kids, right?" She agreed. "And you hate speaking to the board, but I think that your love for the kids is greater than your fear of the board. And you want to overcome this fear, or you wouldn't have let Roy invite me over to talk about the possibility of taking a public speaking class. Is that right?" She nodded slightly.

"You don't know me," I went on, "but I promise you this. If you take my class, you will overcome your fear of speaking and within six months, you'll actually enjoy speaking to groups!"

"Do you want to bet on that last part?" she asked.

"Yes!" I said. She offered no handshake or acknowledgement of a bet, but said, "Where do I show up for classes?"

While Roy wrote out a check for the tuition, I learned more about the couple. He was a wholesale grocery manager accustomed to speaking to groups. Years ago he had even taken a course in public speaking. On the other hand, Diane, an executive with a market research firm, had never had to address a group larger than her staff of three.

When I tried to reach Diane six months after she completed my class, Roy answered the phone, again sounding a little upset. "Oh, Diane is never at home anymore. She's out with another church group showing them how to develop their youth program. She speaks to groups all the time now!"

Next week in the mail I received a card from Diane with just four words on it. *You were right. Thanks!*

Fearless and Persuasive Speaking

Diane was my first student. When we made our bet 10 years ago, I was hoping that my process of instruction would work. Since then — after graduating thousands of executives, managers, salespeople, project managers, teachers, accountants, trainers, engineers, high-school students, doctors, and city officials — I know it does. Beginners quickly become effective speakers, and experienced speakers become even more dynamic communicators.

Many people have shared Diane's feelings at one time or another. I know I did. All of us want our lives to matter, and we want to make a difference by doing something worthy, but getting out of our comfort zone is scary.

The good news is that this sincere desire to make an impact is more powerful than the obstacle of fear. I have witnessed this victory thousands of times. Your fear of public speaking may be as big as a mountain, but it is a mountain that can be climbed. You may be sure you are the only one that is petrified of public speaking, but make no mistake: your fear is universal. You are not alone.

The majority of people feel afraid.

Your feelings of fear place you in the majority, right up there with all the other perspiring men and women standing before their audiences and wondering how they will get through the next few moments without suffering complete humiliation. Guess what? Your anxiety means you are sane. (The only people who *don't* have any fear of public speaking are the poor souls on the sidewalks of major cities who are sermonizing to buildings and passing traffic.)

In fact, I have met only one person in twenty years who said he was never afraid. After watching him speak, it was obvious why. He hid behind the lectern and read every word without risking eye contact. He was not communicating — he was merely reading announcements.

Ken Bradford

*Fear is a natural reaction to moving closer
to the truth.* – Pema Chodron

Everyone wants to avoid painful situations.

The desire to avoid pain is also 100% normal. "Once bitten, twice shy." Through years of training, I have found that *half* the students I talked to could easily recall at least one embarrassing incident that contributed to their present fear of speaking. The other half had fear, but couldn't remember any specific negative experience to explain it.

Either way, it's helpful to realize that everyone has the same fear and that there's nothing wrong with wanting to avoid pain. I suggest you start giving yourself more credit now for facing your problems, and stop trying to figure out the past.

Analysis = paralysis

Past feelings tend to resurface any time we feel threatened — when, for instance, we're asked to speak when we're not prepared, or going on a job interview, or meeting someone we perceive as more powerful than ourselves. When such feelings arise, we can either try to figure out why we feel the way we do (and stay stuck with those feelings) or try to act in a positive, life-changing manner.

I tell my students to quit trying to figure out the "whys" and get busy with the "hows" of public speaking. With the right skills, you can stop dwelling on the past and spend more time building your future. Your need to know "why" can be outgrown.

*You don't change the present by resisting it. The way you
change it is by the creation of new methodologies, which makes
the present obsolete.* – Mike Vance

Accentuate the positive.

It takes just 51% ownership of a corporation's stock to hold a majority — which means you control that company. When you accumulate 51% more positive than negative feelings from speaking to groups, you will have tipped the balance toward more control of your body, mind and message. At that point, as the fear of public speaking begins to lose its hold, you will be able to focus on the positive outcomes that are possible.

Becoming comfortable is not the same as being in total control.

Self-control is important, and control is a goal in effective speaking, but no one has total control. You need to accept feeling more out of control than you would like in the beginning stages of your development. Think about the mounting tension you feel on a roller coaster as you head up the first big incline. When the summit approaches, your stomach hardens, your palms sweat, and you wrap your fingers around the hand bar with the strength of a boa constrictor. Everyone on board is in a heightened state, yet not everyone has panicked — because some have learned not to fear being out of control.

Think of the power of the *Serenity Prayer*: "God grant me the serenity to accept the things I cannot change, the courage to change the things I can, and the wisdom to know the difference." As much as possible, you are trying (*and will be able*) to control three things: 1) your *body*, 2) your *mind*, and 3) your *message*. As you focus on your ability to control that which you *can* control, the factors you cannot control will become less intimidating.

Remember the out-of-control feeling you had while learning to drive a car? Now, years later, you probably drive to work some days, pull into your parking space and wonder how you got there without thinking about the process of driving. The unknowns are still there: pedestrians, other drivers, and the weather. Yet with experience, you have grown comfortable with those variables.

With speaking, the variables come from the audience, the room setup, and your health. Believe it: the sooner you give up the need to feel totally in control before even attempting to speak, the sooner you can start learning how to have control.

> *Life shrinks or expands in proportion to one's courage.*
> – Anais Nin

Fears associated with public speaking

Speaking fears are unique from other fears because the threat is an intangible one. There are no roller coasters or high-speed car crashes, guns, snakes, or IRS auditors present. No real threat of bodily harm exists, but the fear of pain and loss is real. On the inside, though, you're on red alert, because your self-esteem is at risk.

If the situation isn't life threatening, what are we so darn afraid of, anyway? Number one is rejection, because everyone longs to be accepted. Psychologist Abraham H. Maslow prioritized human needs on a hierarchy. High on the list, right after food, clothing and shelter, is the need for acceptance. The phrase, "I could live a week on a sincere compliment," is probably a sign of how important this need is in all of us.

When we speak, we reveal ourselves, expose our vulnerability and risk rejection. As they say in Las Vegas, "Don't fight the house rules." Accept the risk and learn how to play the game.

One favorite client of mine, Southwestern Bell's Helen Morris, came for help after being promoted to a position that required her to teach groups of employees about fiber optics. Helen had been with Bell for twenty-seven years, but never in a management role. "I would rather eat a live tarantula than speak to groups," she told me at the beginning of the class. She wasn't kidding. (You don't hear such an expression often, even in my line of work, but it accurately expresses the intensity of some people's feelings.) After six weeks of coaching, she told me that she "almost" enjoyed speaking to groups.

> *Every submission to our fear enlarges its domain.*
> – Samuel Johnson

But wait a minute! If you feel so uncomfortable, shouldn't you listen to your instincts? No, not always, because the little voice inside you that says, "I'm out of here!" can rule you if you let it. Those who heed its message avoid opportunities to grow and are, as a result, doomed to listen to that little voice echo *another* message for decades to come: "You know you should have pushed yourself a little more back there. Why didn't you try harder?"

Another fear associated with public speaking is embarrassment. I still remember Coach Dickey calling my name from a long list of students who were trying out for cheerleader at McClean Junior High. The audition only required us to run across the stage in front of the student body and yell, "Go Cardinals!" Seconds before my name was called, I peered out from the edge of the stage curtain into a sea of 750 pimply faces. "Next is Kenny Bradford," the coach announced. Panicking, I ran out the stage door across the front lawn of the school. My adrenaline still pumping, I ran around the entire building and jumped into the back row of the auditorium. Unfortunately, the coach was still calling my name. One of my friends had seen me slip in the back, so of course he stood, pointed me out, and yelled to everyone, "Here he is!"

These kinds of old wounds reinforce the conviction that we should avoid all potentially embarrassing situations. They can convince us that *we are different* from everyone else, and that our brand of fear is far greater and more devastating than anyone else's. What's missing is the perspective to see the whole picture. The truth is: your experiences are unique to you, but the feelings that result from them are common to everyone.

Ken Bradford

Fears are hurts that roost in the nest of our memory.
– Robert Schuller

Your subconscious mind stores all your painful memories. When you encounter similar scenarios in the present, those old feelings often resurface. Until past traumas are neutralized, you will become fearful whenever you encounter a risky situation in the present. Eleanor Roosevelt had the right idea when she said, "I must do that which I fear the most." People who overcome the fear of speaking also have painful memories. They have simply learned the right speaking techniques and accumulated more positive experiences than negative.

Remember: when you have a majority of good experiences about speaking, you will no longer be overwhelmed by fear. The fear is not annihilated, but it is conquered. You can focus and go forward. And just as you are not alone in feeling fear, you are not alone in feeling victorious when you conquer it. Millions have learned to defeat fear. So will you.

Ultimately we know deeply that on the other side of every fear lies a freedom. – Marilyn Ferguson

Additional insights

- Our fears are always greater than our real dangers. Most fears bear little relationship to reality.
- Physical exercise helps relax muscles and use up excessive adrenaline.
- Know your subject well. Do extra study or research to make sure you know what you're talking about.
- Refuse to participate in any negative self-talk, like "I'm going to die." Replace it with the truth, " Yes, I am nervous, but I am prepared and I am determined to give it my best!"

- Even if people in the audience know more about the topic than you do, you can still supply new and unique insight.
- Acting incorporates some public speaking skills, speaking incorporates some acting skills — and that's okay. Even managers, salespeople and parents have to "act" sometimes.
- It's better not to eat just before speaking. You want blood for your head, not your Heimlich!
- Any prop can reduce tension by temporarily shifting the spotlight off of you.
- If circumstances allow, ask a good question (as an audience member) before it's your turn to formally present, so you can warm up your vocal cords. (See Chapter 22: Voice.)
- It's best to arrive early to the meeting, unrushed, with a reserve of energy and time.
- Know the room. Become familiar with how your voice sounds in the room. Test it out before the meeting begins. Walk around the meeting room. Practice walking from where you'll be seated to the lectern.
- Believe it or not, 90% of your nervousness is not apparent to the audience, so never tip them off by apologizing.
- You don't have to shrink or swell your ego. Just strive to be your natural self.
- Breathing. Breathing should continue.
- Just because you're experiencing stress doesn't mean you won't make a terrific presentation.

"The reason most people are uncomfortable while speaking is because their focus is on themselves, rather than their message and the audience."
– Steve Allen

TWO

GROWTH

Experience is not the sole factor.

Experience is wonderful, but it never did much for my golf game! Like anything else your speaking ability will improve with time, but it takes more than just experience — it takes, writing, editing, organizing, designing, and some acting skills. Like every art, there is *no one key* to mastering public speaking.

But even knowing these fundamentals isn't enough to turn you into a persuasive, effective speaker. The challenge you face is to utilize the basics (the science) and infuse them with a sense of art (flair) to develop your own unique style.

> *Large challenges always mark the beginning of*
> *new understanding.* – Ralph Lebkuecher

There are many techniques to learn, but growth starts from within. This means getting comfortable, finding your legs, and releasing your personality. Learning to speak well is a process, not an event. Like trees, which grow concentric rings from their core outward, most people develop their natural speaking abilities through a series of successful experiences. Each growth experience consists of four stages:

- First Stage: A motivation to improve and a willingness to try
- Second Stage: A gathering of information
- Third Stage: Practice, Feedback, Coaching, Awareness
- Fourth Stage: Skill development resulting in increased competence

A nurturing, natural approach

Think about it: you've already been using these four stages intuitively all your life to learn new things. As a baby learning to walk, you were *motivated* to reach up for more attractive objects than those found on the floor. Through keen observation, you gathered more *information* about becoming mobile, and you kept practicing until you found your balance. Finally, through encouragement and ever-increasing experience, you mastered the *skill* of walking and were ready for the next learning activity.

You didn't learn how to walk from memorizing how others did it, nor did you learn through goading and repeated embarrassment. Most likely, your parents encouraged you to walk with patience, gentleness, confident verbal messages, and lots of smiling. And that positive teaching environment — full of approval for even your smallest advances — gave you additional motivation. The success rate for this system is most impressive!

A baby contemplating walking, a preschooler contemplating riding a bike, a high school student learning to drive, all of these life challenges present an element of fear, just like public speaking. So why is the approach used by most public school systems and speaking clubs so radically different from this natural learning style that helps us to acquire our necessary life skills and conquer other fears? What happened?

You didn't fail Public Speaking 101. It probably failed you.

High-school speech instructors understand all too well the sheer terror students often feel when asked to speak before their peers. Still, because of the sheer numbers to be educated, they race through textbooks and written exams with little time for individual encouragement, practice and nurturing. Consequently, most people remember high-school speech class not as an enjoyable learning experience, but as a stressful trial they somehow survived. Then later in life, after they've successfully mastered other essential business skills, they wonder why their speaking ability by comparison is so sub-standard.

The wrong kind of help

Toasting clubs attempt to bridge this learning gap, but in these associations, as in high-school speech classes the challenge of fear is rarely properly addressed. The prevailing belief is that everyone has fear, but that writing and delivering speeches will make it go away. Veteran club members will tell you to "get over it." But how?

> *To get good at anything, you must first get comfortable.*
> – Unknown

How many successful professionals can you think of that exhibit extreme nervousness doing their work? How much confidence would you have in a jittery surgeon, defense lawyer, commercial pilot, rock-climbing instructor...? In fact, would you think of anyone clearly in fear of his performance as a *professional*? Would just telling them to "just get over it" help?

There's no substitute for experience, right?

True, if it's a successful experience. But, too many souls have fallen or been pushed into the deep end of the speaking pool and been told to "learn from the experience." Unsuccessful experiences teach a lesson also, and one very difficult to ignore.

The common approach versus the natural approach

Recall how the baby learned to walk in stages: by motivation, by gathering information, by practice/feedback/coaching, and by skill development/repetition. Most toasting clubs follow another approach. For decades, they've maintained their programs using the rigid Robert's Rules of Order agenda, incorporating punishment for correction and negative peer feedback for direction.

To the novice this may sound constructive, but when you are learning a new skill, you don't need public punishment for showing up and trying. Plus, you need a great deal more encouragement than people who are already accomplished. I have met hundreds of people who visited a toasting club for the first time and were startled by some well-meaning officer of the club ringing a bell and pointing out every "uh" as they introduced themselves!

I remember one club in particular, which used a full-size traffic signal with flashing red, yellow, and green lights. Try pretending that's not threatening to the beginner or seriously distracting to everyone else. The most common "corrective measure" seems to be the striking of water glasses with teaspoons by members who hear an "uh" or catch you using what they deem an inappropriate pause. The first time I saw this, it reminded me of my third-grade class performing Christmas carols with borrowed bells.

At these kinds of toasting clubs, more emphasis is placed on speaking with fewer "uhs" instead of speaking naturally. Focusing on the *symptoms* of nervousness like saying "uh" is like treating the symptoms of an illness without alleviating the cause! Over focusing on these symptoms of nervousness takes all the spirit out of people, straitjacketing their spontaneity and dulling their personality. People get taut, not taught. Their delivery becomes stiff and oratorical instead of audience-focused. Many club members do eventually diminish their fear and develop speaking skills, but it's a brutal and lengthy process. The reality is that most visitors never show up for a second meeting.

I have yet to see a want ad seeking managerial candidates who can, make toasts, speak from behind a lectern, and never say "uh." What most companies and associations are looking for are people who can motivate and lead groups. They want leaders who can inspire others by talking *with* their people, not *at* them — individuals who can handle themselves confidently in a variety of business conversations, not just someone who can give a speech.

There is no substitute for persistent effort in the right training atmosphere, where more successes than failures are accumulated in a short period. Ask any physical trainer: with repeated effort under the proper conditions, muscles can be strengthened. Likewise, with self-motivation, encouragement, feedback and experience, your speaking skill level can reach new heights.

Whips or whispers

For centuries, cowboys believed that the only way to break a horse was by using a closed corral, a strong lead and a loud whip. Through control and intimidation, the wrangler worked until the animal's spirit was eventually "broken" enough that he would accept a saddle on his back.

A few years ago a very different method for training horses was popularized. The system utilized more of a nurturing, respectful approach. Instead of breaking the horse's spirit, the cowboy first built a relationship with him. By just talking softly and spending time together, he allowed the horse to overcome its fear of humans. Eventually, the horse accepted a little piece of twine on its back. Trusting the relationship, the horse permitted increasingly larger pieces of cloth placed on its back, until eventually a saddle was allowed.

This nurturing approach to training horses produced a comfortable, natural relationship between horse and rider versus a submissive, passive agreement. Teaching public speaking in line with the second method also produces surprisingly faster growth and greater comfort, resulting in an assertive speaking style that is built on a true connection between speaker and listeners.

Whether it's a baby learning to walk, a young boy struggling to please and impress his father, a grandmother learning to use her computer, or a business executive learning to effectively communicate to groups — humiliation is counter-productive.

We don't need more public speakers. What we need are more good men skilled in speaking. – Quintillion

Additional insights

- Stop searching for the one or two "big keys" to speaking. Focus on skill development, not just knowledge.
- Realize that *practicing* proven techniques is more important than *focusing on all your faults* as a speaker.
- Remember that improvement is rarely linear. Some days, you will feel like you're getting worse at speaking, and that's okay. Remember, a tree's rings may vary in size, but each new ring means it is expanding outward. Apply this growth style to your search for excellence.
- Focus on expressing — not impressing.
- Understand that you will learn best by experiencing frequent successes. Find opportunities to practice speaking often at work and through your trade association.

"There is no deodorant like success." – Elizabeth Taylor
All great speakers were bad speakers first.
– Ralph Waldo Emerson

THREE

VULNERABILITY

Being vulnerable isn't a weakness. It's often a sign of strength.

If someone asked you to name the most powerful character in the Star Wars movies, what would you say? Darth Vadar? If you first thought of the evil antagonist but knew all along it was Yoda, you were right.

Director George Lucas could have introduced the saggy little guy with pointed ears as a nine-foot giant, wearing a majestic robe, hard-plastic ski boots and swinging a twenty-pound saber, but chose not to. Explaining his choice, Lucas said, "If Yoda is really the keeper of the 'Force,' then why would he need all those accessories?" In other words, to dramatize Yoda's true power, he chose to make him *look* vulnerable. Yoda's persona was a brilliant contrast to the macho Rambos and hero-types usually portrayed in movies.

Ken Bradford

Dropping your guard and raising your confidence

If you want to let people perceive you as a confident, self-assured leader, first drop any hint of the cold, steely-faced business look (where you bite your lips slightly, making them appear thin and non-expressive, your eyes are slightly closed, and your jaw is fixed). Although this guarded look is more neutral than offensive, it is not your most confident look. It reminds me of the police motto, "To serve and protect," which is fine for law enforcement, but not the best approach for a public speaker trying to connect with his or her audience. Instead, try to keep your face relaxed, the way it would be while enjoying a conversation with your best friend. (See Chapter 6: Countenance.)

Remember the quiet confidence of Yoda, and abandon the need to defend yourself either physically or emotionally. Sound risky? Yes, but it's an even greater risk coming across as guarded, rigid, or an unapproachable perfectionist.

Carrie was one of my class members who took The Leaders Course® to gain more confidence in communicating with people. She held a successful position as a pension manager for a large medical insurance company. As a child, Carrie had endured the ravages of polio. The disease had left her with a right arm about half the size of her left arm. One evening, in perhaps the fourth session of the training program, she spoke about her experience at a health club the previous weekend. She had finished working out with weights when she noticed the image of herself in a mirror on the wall.

"Normally," Carrie said, "I would never look in a mirror. I didn't want to see myself as I was. But this time I didn't look away. I looked at the whole me, and I accepted what I saw: both the part I didn't like and several parts that weren't so bad!"

That day was a turning point for Carrie, and from then on she spoke and acted more confidently. She quit trying to hide her right arm under her left one. Instead, she started shaking hands with people she met.

She dropped the tiring job of guarding her vulnerable characteristics and started focusing on projecting who she really was. Her talk in class that night challenged all of us to dismantle the walls that were keeping us from outgrowing our self-consciousness.

On the offense

To protect ourselves in uncomfortable situations like public speaking, we sometimes develop habits that make us appear even more uncomfortable. A friend of mine told me he had a good thirty-minute speech, but it only took twenty minutes because he was so nervous.

Talking too fast is one of several unconscious ploys we might use to *keep moving* so no one can harm us. Others are avoiding seriousness, never making eye contact, and gesturing constantly to emphasize every spoken word. These "relief valves" may help you get by, but they only weaken your message.

Accepting your imperfections

When speaking, we are sometimes fighting a battle on two fronts. On one hand we are guarding against being known for *what it is that we don't like about ourselves.* On the other we avoid being noticed for *who we really are.*

But people trust us more when they understand both aspects of our personalities: our logical, analytical side and our emotional side. Accepting, even welcoming, the risk of letting out both realities about ourselves — presenting ourselves as a whole person with strengths and weaknesses — makes our words more acceptable to others. Listeners respond to this vulnerability immediately and positively because they identify with us as a fellow being and not merely as the person who happens to have certain data.

The truth is, any attempt to hide our real selves from our listeners only creates distance from them. What connects speaker to listener is not a convincing pretense, but our obvious, unvarnished essence. Pretending only dilutes our credibility. If we are seen as being less than honest about what is obvious to anyone watching or listening to us, then most of what we say will become questionable. Examining and sharing our adversities is one of the best ways to reveal our real character. (See Chapter 18: Stories.) Instead of hiding your mistakes and imperfections, use them as positive touchstones for connecting with listeners.

> *Tell me the lessons life has taught you and I will be your devoted listener.* – Plato

Leading is risking

Speaking is leading, and leading is always risky. There is no defensive position that eliminates all risk for those who lead. There will always be things we cannot control. Accept it: it's inevitable that at some point, on some occasion, some of your imperfections and faults will show through.

You can eliminate one aspect of the risk of leadership — the agonizing over it. Give yourself permission to be human; to occasionally make a mistake and say, "I was wrong," or "I don't know right now." People will think *more* of you, not less, and will remember your honesty long after they have forgotten the error you made.

Seek improvement, not perfection

Holding yourself up to a faultless standard may seem like a good idea, but it's not. Demanding perfection of yourself only buries your personality, vitality, and uniqueness. Consider Al Gore. Critics and comedians feed off his public appearances, his "stiff" and "wooden" persona. Their criticisms may well strike a painful inner chord with Mr. Gore and only increase his tendency to relate in a cautious manner. (Personally, I think Mr. Gore is intelligent and capable, but he appears to take himself too seriously, especially when speaking to groups.)

Typically, any criticism by others usually only reinforces our fear of being vulnerable and causes us to raise our defensive wall even higher. It is difficult let go of the way we have always done things, especially in the heat of battle. But it's not impossible. Many have learned how.

A successful man is one who can lay a firm foundation with the bricks that others throw at him.
– David Brinkley

Competent ... caring ... approachable

In 1996, presidential candidate Bob Dole showed us only a tough, formal demeanor during his run for the presidency. He spoke just as seriously when describing his hometown — Mission, Kansas — as he did on issues of national security. This constant "grimness" worried voters. If he were elected to the highest office in the world and received even more responsibility, would he behave only as a rigid decision-maker? We want competent leaders, but we also want them to be able to communicate in an approachable, candid, trusting manner.

Five days after losing the election, Mr. Dole was on *The David Letterman Show.* His manner had completely changed. He was relaxed and offered impromptu, candid thoughts. He was the Bob Dole that people from Mission, Kansas, knew. Ironically enough, *that* Bob Dole probably could have won the race. In sharp contrast, his wife, Elizabeth, was the first person on television to step away from the huge fortress stage at the national electoral convention and walk into the crowd. People loved her for it.

Ken Bradford

Preparation

Being vulnerable doesn't mean being under-prepared or disorganized. Being prepared is an important attribute of a professional, and it's essential to be grounded in the key concepts you want to communicate. You need to do your homework, boil your message down to its salient points, practice, and become familiar with the unknowns.

When you've prepared effectively, you know what will be important to the people attending the meeting, and you know how your subject will meet their needs. You will have tested their reaction by talking to a few of them already before your speech, and you know what the first words out of your mouth will be. You are excited, but poised. (See Chapter 13: Preparation.)

The communicator is the person who can make himself clear to himself first. – Paul D. Griffith

Power vs. strength

Mahatma Gandhi cast a fragile shadow, but it was said that when he entered a room you could feel an enormous presence even before seeing him. His quiet confidence came from a mind at peace with a decision, a clear-cut objective, and a commitment to a cause bigger than himself. Gandhi's inner strength galvanized his listeners' attention. When he spoke, his voice conveyed the power of refined ideas and convictions derived from first-hand experience. He had thought carefully about his message and condensed it to just three repeatable words: "You are free." Anyone in India at that time of British rule could have used the same three words, but Gandhi's demeanor gave them impact. His message ignited listeners like a wildfire invading dry grassland.

Like the small stone in David's sling, faith is a mighty thing. – Dedra Watts

What the world's most influential leaders knew

World-shaping religious leaders like Jesus, Mohammed, and Buddha understood the power of vulnerability. None was ever depicted with a scowl or with his arms crossed over his chest. Instead they are remembered with open arms and gentle faces. While vulnerable to those with swords, their persuasive skills and leadership abilities gave them the power to move the masses.

The civil rights conflicts in the 1960s could have been much more destructive if Martin Luther King, Jr. had not preached a philosophy of non-violence. He taught the power of vulnerability. Before each public demonstration, he told followers, "If there is to be blood in the streets, let's make sure that it is our blood." He foresaw how the nation would respond to brutality against vulnerable protesters.

Of course there were other options, and dissenters opposed his strategy. Still, as history records, asserting a strong message while being vulnerable proved to be the best tactic.

A time for an extreme offense

George Patton was a flamboyant general. His aggressive nature was needed in World War II when the best and only defense was a strong offense. (Lincoln probably would have loved having Patton at the head of the Army of the Potomac.) In that emergency, his take-charge, kick-down-the-door style would have been just right. In peacetime, however, such aggressive leadership is as out of place as a Sherman tank in the employee parking lot. At times, business may look like war, but the troops are not as restricted. They have the right to choose their leaders.

I suppose that leadership at one time meant muscle; but today it means getting along with people.
– Indira Gandhi

Ken Bradford

Take a lesson in vulnerability from the richest and most powerful person on daytime television, Oprah Winfrey. Does she hide behind a lectern? She probably doesn't even own one. And Oprah knows about tough critics. She handles them beautifully, because she doesn't see the need to fight. Instead, she acknowledges her personal challenges openly, honestly and with a sense of humor, which usually melts the barrels of those ready to shoot her down.

Mastering transparency

With enough successful experience in public speaking, you will achieve a kind of transparency, so that what the audience remembers is not just you being yourself, or how you gestured, or the background color of your slides, but the ideas that you have clearly conveyed. You become secondary, while your *ideas* become primary. They are what you want the audience to remember.

Think of yourself as simply the tool that delivers the message. In the acting world, it is the discovery of truth or the moment of tragedy that moves an audience, not what the actors are wearing. In music, it is the shared feeling between performer and listener that makes for applause, not the instrument. In emergencies, it is the *cry for help* that breaks through preoccupation, not *who* is crying out. In sales, it is the relevant benefit to the customer that sells the deal, not the salesman's hand-painted tie.

Remember, if you can leave your protective ego at the door, your ideas will have a chance of coming across. The key is to remember to put the audience's needs ahead of your own need to protect yourself.

May the internal and the external person be as one.
– William Shakespeare

The right physical message

These outer, physical suggestions are mentioned last because vulnerability must be mastered from within.

Posture: Open, relaxed. Strong upright body. Shoulders slightly back, but not pulled backward like a soldier at attention. The head is directly above the neck rather than protruding forward and over the chest. Your ankles are uncrossed and your weight is equally balanced. Avoid shifting uncomfortably from side-to-side, signaling a need to flee!

Arms and fingers should do what they normally do when you're totally relaxed — they hang at our sides. This will feel extremely unnatural to you if you are accustomed to always keeping your elbows bent, but after a short while, you will enjoy the extra energy this saves. You wouldn't buy a used car from someone with clenched fists, nor would you buy ideas from a person speaking with combat-ready knuckles.

Face: Open, looking assured without tightness. Imagine yourself as an idling racecar. You could accelerate in a blur. Within seconds you could be at mach speed if you wanted. You look confident, not cocky.

Gestures: Wide and large enough to match the size of your ideas and the breadth of the audience.

Remaining vulnerable

To summarize, we are all born vulnerable. We learned how to protect ourselves, and our methods became habits. It is difficult to reveal ourselves to others, especially those we do not know. It takes practice, but we can do it if we remember the importance of our message, subdue the desire to distinguish ourselves, and try to stay on an equal footing with our audience.

Additional insights

- Continue striving to be your bravest self. If you had always taken refuge in your comfort zone, would you be where you are today?
- The biggest risk is not allowing others to know your uniqueness.
- Dare to be the "genuine article:" the person your friends and family admire.
- Know that your confidence in yourself is a silent force, working invisibly to your advantage.
- Offer your sincerity, conviction, common sense and heart to all who hear you speak. They may not always agree, but they are sure to hear your message.

FOUR

CONNECTING

If the speaker can't connect, the listeners will disconnect.

There's a gap between speaker and audience that the effective communicator will bridge right away. Being aware of this gap will help you to connect better with your listeners. The goal: bridge the gap and maintain a conduit of understanding between you and the listeners. Communicating is a two-way process, involving both delivering and receiving. In addition to broadcasting a message, you're also paying attention to how it arrives. Your communication style should resemble a satellite that both transmits and receives signals. The result: listeners will feel like you are talking *with them* rather than *at them.*

Occasionally I meet someone who boasts, "I never have a problem speaking to groups. I know my presentation really well and I don't care what people think." But feeling great about your ability and qualifications doesn't guarantee that your audience is listening. If your audience doesn't listen to your message, your knowledge of the subject is inconsequential.

Decades ago, information was not as accessible or plentiful as it is today. Modern audiences are overwhelmed with information and forced to be far more selective with their time. They demand data that is highly relevant, interesting, beneficial, or entertaining.

Of course, there are no guarantees that an audience will listen to you, but you can apply the Golden Rule: Audiences are more likely to pay favorable attention to you if you pay attention to them. You can take steps to help ensure audience interest by surveying their goals and challenges, conducting interviews, or researching their background before you speak with them.

Consider the difference between novice and pro ice skaters. The novice focuses on connecting and reconnecting with the ice. So does the pro, but the pro also connects with the audience.

You've suffered through enough speakers who don't relate to their audiences: the teacher who drones on and on, the minister who lectures to a half-asleep congregation, the manager who reads safety regulations to his daydreaming workers. Many people accept these situations as being "normal" because they are common. However, if you ignore a fidgety, foot-tapping audience that is gazing out the window, you run the risk of having them completely check out on you.

Can you really do a better job at reaching your audience than an experienced minister or a highly educated professor? Absolutely. It's not that difficult if you practice and use the following techniques:

Eye contact. Consider these tips:
- **Look into the faces** of the audience members. If you aren't comfortable doing that, practice on one person for a few moments and move on. However, don't shift your attention at regular intervals or you might look robotic, like a lawn sprinkler.

- **Don't make the mistake** of focusing only on the friendly-looking fellow in the front row and ignoring everyone else. Think like a trial lawyer talking to a jury. In other words, every person who hears you speak can give you a vote, and every vote counts.
- **Avoid spending too much time** trying to win someone over who obviously doesn't care for you or what you are communicating.
- **Try not to talk primarily to one side of the room,** even if you feel more comfortable with that side. Instead, try to divide your eye contact equally among all sections of the audience. (See Chapter 10: Involvement.)

Keep in mind that *you* are also the message. Your body language, reactions, and appearance send powerful signals while you speak. For example, what assumption do you make about a speaker who smoothes his hair, adjusts his tie, and hurriedly puts on his jacket as he rushes to the podium? Probably that he is unprepared, self-conscious, and unsure of himself…not the message you want to send. (See Chapter 11: Visuals.)

Never talk down to the audience. Of course, no one deliberately patronizes an audience. It tends to happen when a speaker feels threatened or tries to sound like an authority — as, for instance, when a new manager, who feels intimidated, is talking to more experienced personnel. The speaker may be trying to sound like an authority on a subject, but actually be coming across as a lecturing judge.

Mark Smith (not his real name), a commercial real estate agent, recently asked me to listen to his presentation to the board of directors of a highly successful national retail operation. Although Mark's facts were organized and logical, he was frequently challenged and interrupted during his presentation. He later admitted to me that he was a little "uptight" in front of this particular audience. Although they were casually dressed and friendly, almost every audience member had a net worth of several million dollars.

I asked Mark to repeat his response to the first question from the audience. He said he had told the questioner, "You're wrong." To another challenge on a topic he knew well, he responded, "You're missing my point." By going through a little role reversal with me, he was able to understand how negative he had sounded to his listeners. As he played the part of the audience, he saw clearly what kind of a critical and threatening impression he had made.

Mark realized that he needed a new approach. Instead of, "You're missing the point!" he omitted the criticism and started trying to understand the listener's point. Rather than saying, "You're wrong!" he tried, "How do you mean?" or "Could you help me understand your point better?" He still may not have agreed with their point, but he increased his chances of solving the differences, and he let the other person save face.

Remember: Correcting someone in public is not forbidden, and at times it may be necessary, but you run the risk of them doubling their resistance to your ideas. Unless you must correct someone, like when a fact is misrepresented, like an incorrect number, date, or name, try to avoid doing so. Even then, you might want to say, "I *believe* it is…" rather than say, "It is." As Benjamin Franklin once said, "I made it a rule to forbear all direct contradiction to the sentiments of others."

Don't act like a parent. In his book *Games People Play,* Dr. Eric Berne reminds us how we can sometimes take on a parental role to make a point when we're under stress. Guilty as charged! I've experienced this firsthand.

One night my two kids were playing Monopoly on the living room floor when I came home from a long night teaching a class of adults. When I walked in, the kids asked me to play. I said, "Sure," and sat down. Both began giving me money from their piles because they had distributed the bank's money between them. All of the money! There was no "bank."

Upon seeing this, I said with great authority, "This isn't how you play! Do you want me to read you the rules here on the box top?"

As I picked up the lid, they both screamed, "Dad! This is the way we play! Do you want to play or not?"

That incident made me more aware of my communication style. If I wanted to play with them, I had to get on a child-to-child level. After all, it was just a game. Following that incident, I became more aware of the need to speak with adults on an adult-to-adult level, too. Business isn't a child's game. And sounding like a parent who's talking down to your children when you're speaking to a business audience is a sure-fire way to alienate them.

Take a tip from Dr. Stephen Covey, the author of several highly regarded books, including *The Seven Habits of Highly Successful People*. When he's teaching, he says, "How am I doing? Am I explaining this well?" instead of, "Do you get it?" or, "Do you understand me?" As the leader, *he* takes the responsibility for clearly communicating his message.

Keep the audience's purpose in mind. What motivates them? Are they here by choice or because they have to be? If their attendance has been coerced, you may want to acknowledge that fact in a tactful manner so the audience won't continue to be preoccupied with a negative thought. What do they need to learn or understand? Focus on their needs and the beneficial messages you want them to leave with, and plan your presentation accordingly.

Start and end on time. You can deduct five minutes of speaking value for every one minute a preacher goes over his allotted time. If a speaker runs long, you *may* hear his words, but your primary focus will be on lunch!

Where's the common ground? We identify with others who are like us, who have similar interests, experiences, values, concerns, etc. The sooner you can identify the common ground between you and your audience, the better. What do you have in common? Consider using an appeal to the higher, nobler motives of all human beings, like determination, love, persistence, creativity, passion, family, friends, accomplishment, etc. We all want our children to be happy and healthy. We all want to live in a safe neighborhood. Remember, "common" is the root word of "communicating."

Use stories to relate. (See Chapter 18: Stories.) People identify with characters in stories who must deal with the forces of good and evil. As they get swept up in the characters' feelings, they will feel their own emotions begin to stir, especially if they are rooting for the underdog.

Occasionally, go inward to connect. It has been said that nothing is more universally bonding between speaker and audience than the act of sharing a reflective, impromptu thought. This happens when we break away from the planned text and share what we are thinking at the moment. For example, wouldn't it be nice to occasionally hear a politician say something like, "Let me think how I feel about that," instead of giving a canned reply.

Sometimes you'll see performers stop the regular program and offer a peek behind the scenes or tell of something that happened "minutes before the show." Yes, this can be a risky technique, but also rewarding on the connection scoreboard. Warning: The inward thought you are sharing with the group should never be critical or condemnatory of anyone besides yourself.

Summing up. Connecting is about understanding that the unconscious messages you are sending and receiving from your audience are just as important as your verbal message. Good speaking focuses not only on how you manage your own feelings, but also on the feelings of the group.

Connecting means being aware not only of *what* you have to say, but *how* you say it, and *how* you look when you say it...especially your facial language. (See Chapter 6: Countenance.)

It also means learning to see the bigger picture beyond the words, just as your audience does. Connecting is entirely up to you. As the speaker, as the leader, take responsibility for connecting with an *effective presentation,* not just for "giving speeches."

> *When we blame, we give up our ability to change.*
> – Steve Straus

Additional insights

- Emotions are often easier to understand than words or numbers. If you sincerely feel pride or enthusiasm, let it show. If you're not moving your audience's emotions in some way, why bother continuing? You might as well mail your remarks to them.
- Watch your voice level. Too soft a voice is usually interpreted as disinterest on your part. (See Chapter 9: Energy and Chapter 22: Voice.) If you are concerned about being too loud, you could simply come early and test the equipment.
- If it's a toss-up whether to use a positive or negative example to make your point, go with the negative one. People often pay more attention to strife and disappointment than to good news. (Unfortunately, television news producers make great use of this phenomenon.)
- Avoid unproductive pauses (not to be confused with pauses for effect as in Chapter 19: Persuasion.) Your audience will unplug mentally just the way they change channels when nothing's happening on the television set.
- Remember that your *desire* to connect is crucial in achieving a connection. Try. Everyone will appreciate your effort.

FIVE

MOVEMENT

Move. Be more than a talking head.

The white-haired lady ahead of me in the supermarket check-out line was showing me a photograph. "This is my grandson Paul. He's captain of his soccer team," she said. Cupped in her hand was a picture of a young kid holding a soccer ball.

"I would be proud of him, too," I told her.

The line moved again and she returned the photo to her purse. Our encounter had lasted only a few seconds, but that was enough time to look at a single picture. Obviously, if it had been possible for her to show me a ten-second video clip of Paul zigzagging a determined path through six larger defenders and scoring the winning goal, it would have better captured my interest and for a longer time. The point is, a still photo is similar to a mostly motionless speaker. Neither commands prolonged attention.

People like action. Action is the magical ingredient that makes television, stage plays, television news reports, films, and MTV immensely more popular than radio. Radio isn't visual and can't show us animation, so we usually find something unrelated to do while it's on — like driving, dancing or cleaning house. Remember: as a speaker or leader of a group, you can't afford to have your audience doing something unrelated while you're delivering a message.

When and how to move, and how often. This depends first on whether your movement has a purpose. You might want to enhance meaning by making your movements and gestures larger or more dramatic, like walking over to the projection screen and tapping your fingers next to the number on the bottom line. To add clarity to your message, you might want to act it out a little. For example, if you are talking about how much more important it is to wear a smile than to wear a smiley badge, you could wear the badge, point to it and then point to your face. Those are purposeful movements.

Purposeless movements are ineffective gestures and body language that distract the listener or barely emphasize your spoken words. They do have a purpose, but it is not what you want. Arms and legs are moved to use up adrenaline. When we are anxious, we want to take flight or stay and fight something. Our bodies are geared up even if we know rationally that there is no real threat. So we move out of discomfort because we need to do something with our extra energy. Think of people who continually shift their weight from side to side, or speakers who rock forward on one foot and then back on the other. Motions like these may decrease your stress, but they can add to the discomfort of those obliged to listen to you.

Where the eye goes — the mind flows.

Congruent movement is the goal. Your listeners should be so captivated by your message — and its delivery — that they are not consciously aware of your gestures and body movements. It's when your body language is incongruent, and doesn't match what is spoken, that listeners will focus on what your body is saying instead of your words.

Use a variety of moves. The enemy is predictability. When your actions become predictable, the audience begins to tune you out. Our brains get bored watching assembly-line movements for more than a minute. We would rather look away and listen than be hypnotized against our will. If heads in the audience start to bow or eyes look out the window, you may need to introduce a change. (See Chapter 15: Variety.)

Seven ways to add physical movement to create positive variety:

1. Step out from behind the lectern and stand beside it.
2. Walk over to a flipchart or whiteboard and draw something.
3. While speaking, walk to one side of the room for a few moments. Later, walk to the other side to get closer to listeners and improve eye contact.
4. Step to the very front of the stage area and speak. Be careful not to walk so far forward that some in the front row can only see your side view.
5. Walk to a prepared poster. Flip it over to the prepared side and hold it high enough for everyone to see.
6. Walk to the front row and hand an audience member a prop to be passed around.
7. Raise your hand and ask the audience a question. Out-stretch one hand as if you are catching their response.

Movement increases drama, humor, sincerity, pride, and disappointment. The more dimensions you can bring to an audience, the more experienced and real you appear to them. Like a diamond large enough to carry many facets, you increase your value by being multi-dimensional.

Using your hands

For years, I never knew what to do with my hands while speaking to groups. One teacher told me to use them as if I were hugging a Volkswagen; another suggested I put them in my pockets. How was I supposed to learn the right way when everyone disagreed?

One book said that nervous people should hold their hands at their sides and pinch their thumbs into the tips of their fingers. For two years I thought this was working — until someone came up and told me I looked like Buddha. Then I tried keeping my hands moving, the old "gravity defiance" method. I emphasized everything. If I told you the time, I used both hands. I've tried the other extreme too, nailing my arms to my sides, which gave me the look of someone in a straitjacket, or what other people have called the headless horseman image. Since the so-called experts could only tell me what not to do, I stayed pretty much lost-in-space on what to do and when.

Over time, I learned that there are three hard and fast rules for using hand gestures.

1. **Your hands should emphasize your message, not distract from it.** Allow them to complement your words. If you're not using them, let them rest. When they're truly resting, they hang down naturally from your shoulders with no tension or nervous movement. As logical as this sounds, it can feel very unnatural at first. My initial reaction was, "This can't be right, because keeping my hands moving feels better than letting them hang there lifeless when I'm not using them."

Fearless and Persuasive Speaking

You'll have to decide, as I did, what is more important: delivering an effective message or doing what feels good! It's like the challenge you face getting out of bed on cold mornings, when your first inclination is to stay in bed and stay warm under the sheets. Sleeping in is the most comfortable thing to do, but it's not the best way to collect a paycheck. Likewise, learning to let your hands rest when they're not in use feels like another uncomfortable problem at first, but it's ultimately your best course of action. Gesturing from a point of stillness is also more dramatic.

2. **Enlarge your gestures as your group size expands.** Recently, the president of a large medical firm spoke to about fifty people. In a near monotone, he said, "We are all really thrilled with the 25 million dollar acquisition." As he spoke, both his thumbs remained on the lectern and his fingers lifted briefly like the last flap of a dying pigeon. It was a million-dollar announcement with a two-dollar gesture. He could have used at least a quarter million dollar gesture to make us believe he was thrilled!

   You don't always need elaborate multimedia presentations to make a huge impact. You can just be yourself — made larger.

   In another failed attempt to control my own hands, I have tried to restrict the size of my gestures by keeping them small and close to the middle of my body. This is especially dangerous when you get behind a lectern. It causes listeners to imagine you doing something else with your hidden hands, such as rolling pie dough, or worse.

3. **There are no wrong gestures, only gestures used at the wrong time.** For example, holding both hands over your crotch and smiling may be quite appropriate for your first visit to a nudist resort, but it's less than impressive in front of a panel of urologists. Similarly, wild hip gyrations, while

slapping your thigh with your hand might be a little much for your department meeting on sexual harassment, but it could be great for teaching third-base coaches.

Similarly, folding your arms to look contemplative or putting one hand in your pocket and shifting your weight to one side to show you're relaxed is not always a bad thing. It all depends on the situation and the message you are trying to convey. Just know your audience and what message your gestures are sending. And if you do put your hand in your pocket, stop gesturing with that hand!

Hands are powerful communicators, often more revealing about what's going on inside us than the words we offer. Strive to let them reflect your poise and confidence in yourself and your message. It's a skill you can learn by practicing these three rules.

The brain is more slowly stirred by the ear
than by the eye. – Voltaire

Movements (or positions) to avoid

Standing up hesitantly. Don't rise cautiously from your chair like an accused person anticipating a guilty verdict. When it's time to stand, rise smoothly and confidently without telegraphing any signs of nervousness. Look like you are glad that the group called on you, even if you're thinking the opposite.

Getting dressed on the way to the front. First impressions begin long before you reach the front of the room. If you want your coat buttoned or your waistband higher, take care of it before you stand. (See Chapter 11: Visuals.)

Rocking or shifting your weight from side to side. This isn't completely wrong. It just distracts, especially when the audience starts placing bets on your next shift.

Out-of-paper-towels finger-flicking. Emphasizing every ... single ... spoken ... word by dropping the hands and wrist as you speak. Where there is over emphasis, there is no emphasis.

Cat-clock eyes. Eyes that shift repetitively from side to side without ever really looking at anyone in the audience.

The dry wash. Rubbing the hands together using invisible soap and water.

The "I don't really mean it" stance. Crossing the legs at the ankles, while letting the head drop to one side. It's a sign of submission and weakness — half of a curtsy. In business presentations, it screams, "I'm tired, bored, giving in," or all the above.

Key executive. Playing with keys, coins and other things that rattle in your pockets. One sure cure is to empty your pockets first.

Buddha. Achieved by keeping the arms at the sides and pressing the thumb and pointing finger into each other to form a circle. Ideally, you want to release all tension from your fingers and let them hang naturally when not using them.

Space is power

Odds are, the biggest office in your company belongs to the president. Why? Is it because he or she needs more room to do more work? Probably not. More likely it is because a big office demonstrates power.

Professional singers and actors, who are required to project their presence, know how to make use of space. You probably don't want to look like a rock star or television evangelist or opera singer — but you can study their techniques.

In speaking, when people use more space, they expand their presence. All you have to do is have a purpose for moving, and then try to occupy more of the area up front. Simply standing instead of remaining seated or walking over to the marker board, flipchart, front table, projection screen, or briefly down the front aisle might accomplish this.

Show what you mean. Get excited. Open up. Audiences want to see your commitment. When you're in action, listeners are more likely to want to get into action. Space is free and almost always available. If you are moving with a purpose, and not just for show, your message will have greater impact.

Ken Bradford

I would rather see a preacher look like he was fighting bees than one that just looked like a talking head.
– Abraham Lincoln

Additional insights

-   Only movements with purpose, add emphasis to your verbal message. The rest can dilute it.
-   Demonstrating the idea often adds more understanding and believability than only hearing the same idea.
-   Avoid holding pens, keys, or other objects in your hands while you're speaking. Don't use the marker to show off your juggling ability.
-   Carrying brief notes in your hand is usually fine. Use your free hand to do most of the gesturing, which is more expressive than shaking and waving notepaper.
-   Purposeful movement signifies that your focus is on delivering the message and not on yourself.
-   Our hands are the extremities of our thoughts. Although silent, they speak volumes about our inner state.

SIX

COUNTENANCE

**A neutral countenance communicates an
apathetic or negative attitude.**

Early on, listeners may not know what you are going to say,
but if they look at you, they already know how you feel about
it. Your facial expression telegraphs your intent.

Let go of the idea that you need to always wear a deadpan
business face to be taken seriously as a credible businessperson.
It's like wearing a mask, and hiding behind it. If you want your
audience to be enthusiastic, you must project enthusiasm: and to
do that, you must communicate your feelings.

Look like you mean what you say. The director of a large software firm tells his shareholders, "We are really looking forward
to an exciting fourth quarter." This sounds good on paper, but
from a listener's perspective he looks like he has just said, "We

have some less expensive caskets in the basement, if you prefer." His voice says, "exciting," but his face says, "I hope your day is as miserable as mine." He has bought into the myth that smiling will kill his "professional look."

Inspire confidence. When John F. Kennedy stepped onto the lawn of the White House Rose Garden to announce the blockade of Cuba, most Americans thought we were on the edge of World War III. Flashing a big grin at that moment would have been inappropriate, as would have been exhibiting out-of-control rage. Kennedy's slight smile, however, radiated confidence and calm resolve.

Months after the crisis had passed, during a newspaper interview, Kennedy frankly admitted how nervous he had been during that stressful time. Had he let his face reflect his own personal uncertainty, he might have compromised the security of the Free World. Instead he displayed a poise that complemented his message and reassured a fearful nation.

Kennedy knew that not only was all of America watching him: the leaders of the Soviet Union were also evaluating his demeanor for any signs of doubt, fear, or uncertainty. They didn't see any — and the Russian ships subsequently returned to Russia.

Of all the things you wear, your expression is most noticeable.
– Confucius

I am not suggesting you wear a Ronald McDonald clown smile to a funeral. Yet even in times of extreme sorrow, mourners will sometimes offer an understanding smile to friends and family. Surprisingly, the person whose loss is greatest and who was closest to the deceased may greet you with a beautiful smile that says that despite his or her loss, he or she has found some peace during a difficult time.

If you want to look natural, look like you're at peace with the moment. After all, inward peace is our natural state. Stress is something we have learned to wear. With awareness and practice we can overcome it.

A deadpan face results in a monotone voice. Businesspeople usually talk about sales, profits and service, not life and death issues. But when it comes time for them to speak, too many of them take themselves and their subject far too seriously. A dead-pan face forces the voice to emerge through a tight exterior, which in turn narrows the sound range. Few people actually speak in a monotone, but many slip into that narrow vocal range after they stand to speak. Displaying a flat, expressionless face will never bring your words to life.

> *Good acting requires some speaking skills.*
> *Good speaking requires some acting skills.*

Methods for adding expression to your expressions

Practice making your face look ALIVE:

A   Attentive, alert, animated (not stagnant), in the moment

L   Listening to the audience as you speak. Your face must look open to the reaction of others.

I   Interested in the topic.

V   Vibrantly active. Your face changes slightly as it adds subtle nuances to the meaning of your words. Your eyes don't have that deer-in-the-headlights look, your jaw shouldn't remind the audience of a puppet, and both your lips move when you speak, not just the lower one. Your eyebrows, cheeks and forehead all add emphasis at appropriate moments.

E   Enthusiastic. (From the Greek word, entheos, inspired) A force that attracts and persuades.

Ken Bradford

Barriers

Anything that comes between you and the observer can block expression and become a handicap. The more of these barriers you have surrounding your face, the more you will want to compensate for their influence:

Eyeglasses. Strategy: Raise your eyebrows slightly higher than you normally would so they can be seen above the rims. Consider wearing contact lenses on the days that you present.
Mustache or beard. Strategy: Keep hairline trimmed above the top lip. Raise cheeks when smiling.
Large stationary microphone on a lectern. Strategy: Ask for a hand-held, cordless microphone, which you can hold below your chin or use a lavaliere mike clipped to your lapel.
Stress-induced scowl. Strategy: Just before you speak, think of one of the happiest moments of your whole life and take your expression up front with you.

Such is human psychology that if we don't express our joy, we soon cease to feel it. – Lin Yutang

Another method for improving your non-verbal message includes critiquing yourself on videotape. You can also ask a trusted friend to give you feedback on your usual expression(s) when speaking to a group.

The countenance you display has a lot to do with what will be reflected back to you. In other words, you should work on projecting whatever it is you want from your listeners first. If it's more commitment, acceptance, enthusiasm, or involvement, show them first with your facial expressions that you are committed, accepting, enthusiastic, or involved. At first, you might have to do a little acting to form the habit, but what's wrong with trying to act like your best self in front of others? Eventually it will become second nature.

[60]

Fearless and Persuasive Speaking

Remember, the expression you show to others is never set in stone: it's up to you to choose. You can react to the stress of speaking, or you can act out of faith in yourself. Try letting your best thoughts show on your face. It will help attract others to your thinking and influence those around you to follow.

A poker face is fine for hiding how you feel in a game of cards, but if you're playing a leadership role, it seldom wins you a hand.

Most people are about as happy as they make up their minds to be. – Abraham Lincoln

Additional insights

- Smile more. You owe it to your face and to your friends.
- It is easier to act your way into a better feeling than feel your way into action.
- Audiences/employees often look to you initially to see how happy they should be.
- When you're under pressure, you may have to remind yourself (or have someone else remind you) to smile.
- Before entering the meeting room, try yawning to flex your facial muscles.
- Your face usually communicates your feelings. It's also your personal trademark.
- You look your best when your face reflects joy.

"A kind countenance is a double presence."
– Thomas Fuller

SEVEN

RAPPORT

Rapport is the strongest connection.

Humiliation is a cruel teacher. I once gave a presentation to an audience that spoke and understood only Japanese. I was an exchange student in Hiroshima, Japan, and had been asked to speak to the Lion's Club. The day before the event I wrote a one-page speech expressing how happy I was to be their guest. I wanted my speech to go really well, so I asked my Japanese host, Haruo, to translate it. Then I asked him to read it back to me slowly in his language. As Haruo said the words in Japanese, I wrote them down in phonetic English, filling the page. I was up all night memorizing those sounds.

The moment of truth came the next day as I stood up to give my memorized speech. I uttered the first four phonetic sounds and promptly went blank. Panicking, I searched for my "cheat sheet" but couldn't find it. As I looked up in humiliation and defeat, the audience bowed their heads, acknowledging my disgrace. In the front row, one man said to another, "Another American bomb!"

Real truths are realized, not memorized.

The truth was, I couldn't speak Japanese, and I couldn't trick the audience into thinking I had learned their language overnight. By avoiding what I thought was a shortcoming, I was reciting instead of speaking normally. I was giving it my best, but your "best shot" is sometimes not enough, especially in building rapport. You must also have the right techniques to succeed.

Rapport is the process of revealing two personalities: yours and the audience's.

You create rapport whenever an audience responds to a real emotion you have shared with them, whether it's frustration, love, or joy. It's not enough to tell them what you're feeling: you must let them share in the experience of feeling the emotion. If the experience and the feelings that you had about it are sincere and authentic, your audience will relate to it, because feelings are universal.

Trust is a powerful ingredient of rapport.

Trust that an example from your own background will be effective. By personalizing your story, you're showing confidence that the audience will accept you as a person. Speaking in a revealing way (without embarrassing yourself), helps the audience trust you, which increases their participation and commitment. (See Chapter 19: Persuasion.)

All power is trust. – Benjamin Disraeli

We are all selling trust.

Audiences give their trust the same way you and I do: by evaluating a person's words and body language, and by listening to the sound of their voices. Sincerity has a ring to it. You'll know you have established rapport and built trust when the audience enjoys your presence. You'll see it in their faces and relaxed posture. They literally loosen up and become more open. Here are more keys:

1. **If *you* want the audience to accept you, give *them* acceptance as soon as possible.** Use your eyes, face, and the warmth of your voice. If you need more warmth, focus more on sincerity, and praise your audience with enthusiasm!
2. **Use open body posture.** Avoid clasping your hands together for very long. This creates a barrier between you and the audience and discourages spontaneous, free gestures. You want to encourage a safe environment where everyone's ideas can be heard without judgment. Your body language and posture must reflect this acceptance and openness. Remember: Real communications doesn't begin until people feel safe.
3. **Engage listeners** through short rhetorical questions such as: "Right?" "You know?" or "Make sense?" Using short rhetorical questions and acknowledging their responses will tell you if you're in synch with your audience.

By definition, communication means two-way communication.
Insecure individuals don't like it.
Bosses don't like it. Leaders and innovators do.
– Mark Shepherd, Chairman, Texas Instruments

4. **Be flexible.** Don't memorize your speech. Allow yourself to be stretched. Reading a talk is about as persuasive as a salesperson reading a script to a prospect. Reading from slides is

making the same mistake. You must connect in a human way. Even the most formal speaker can usually improve with a little ad-libbing.

5. **Create a dialogue with listeners.** Listen attentively, and then respond back to the audience's reactions. Show awareness of their presence.

6. **Talk in terms of *their* interests and needs.** Socrates once said, "Talk to me about *me* and I will be your devoted listener."

7. **Create a survey of the future audience, before your next meeting.** Make it brief and easy to complete and return to you. Even if you're speaking to a group of only three or four people, you'll be more on target with their needs and thought processes and they will feel more important and appreciated.

Audiences have a natural urge to connect with a speaker. They welcome friendly interaction. And when they feel motivated to participate, you both win. (See Chapter 10: Involvement.)

The speaker who knows how to create rapport is like an orchestra leader who can direct each section of his ensemble to produce a powerful melody. It is an invaluable tool for any leader to cultivate.

The truth of a thing is in the feel of it, not the think of it.
– Stanley Kubrick

Additional insights

-   If an audience recognizes that you've worked hard on their behalf to prepare, you'll build rapport.
-   Understand the audience's jargon (the language of the audience). Don't try to pass yourself off as an expert on their subject, but be familiar with enough key terms to show your interest. People relate to those who take some time to get to know them. Find at least one inside understanding, so you

can personalize your text to your listener's interest.

- Use a little self-effacing humor to personalize your talk and get the audience on your side.
- If you are at all honored to speak to a group, tell them so, but give them a specific reason why. Your audience won't believe a trite expression like "I'm really glad to be here," or "It's a great honor to speak with you," unless you also give them a specific and sincere follow-up reason.

EIGHT

EYE CONTACT

Good eye contact is as important with a group as it is one-on-one.

Meeting the eyes of so many people all at once may be intimidating, but it can't be avoided, because communication with an audience doesn't really begin until the speaker makes good eye contact.

The face is the mirror of the mind, and eyes without speaking confess the secrets of the heart.
–Saint Jerome

What if you were talking with someone about buying his house and he never looked at you? How would you feel about the transaction? Would you feel you were getting the whole truth about the house? Probably not, because poor eye contact lowers credibility.

By looking at your audience and acknowledging their presence, you are establishing a physical and emotional connection with them Think about how alienated you, as a speaker, would feel if no one in the audience looked at you. (For that matter, think of the frustration you feel in restaurants when the waiter seems to be avoiding your eyes.)

In today's competitive business environment, credibility is all important, and no one can afford to look dishonest or detached. Still, making eye contact can be tough when you're self-conscious. (See Chapter 3: Vulnerability.) To make it easier, try to stop focusing on yourself and instead concentrate on the audience and your message. Here are some ideas to help refocus your energy:

1. Give listeners what they want. Audiences want to be accepted as much as you do. With any audience, what we give is usually what we get. Acknowledge them with your eyes as soon as you are introduced, or when you start the meeting. This sets the tone for what will follow and is tantamount to saying, "I notice you. You are important to me. I'm glad you are here." Why do you suppose retailers encourage employees to greet the customer as soon as he or she walks into a store? Because they know that this acknowledgment creates a sense of importance in their customers that translates into more purchases. The same truth applies when you are speaking and "selling yourself." Make sure the audience knows you accept them, and chances are they will accept you, too.

2. Become more interested in your information. Enthusiasm is contagious. Get excited about what you are saying. Dig a little deeper than necessary into your topic and become so involved in sharing what you have found that you forget your fear of looking into the audience's eyes. Don't worry about being *impressive*. Concentrate on *expressing*. Your improved eye contact will flow naturally from your desire to connect.

3. Benefits, benefits, benefits. Here is an old advertising adage: Sell benefits, not features. If you know why the audience should listen to you — how they will benefit from hearing what you have to say — you'll feel more relaxed and straightforward while addressing them. Everyone feels empowered when they are helping someone else. If you don't know how the audience will benefit from what you're saying, you probably shouldn't be standing in front of them!

4. Slow down. Don't rush through the presentation as if it's a five-minute fire drill. You don't have to fill every gap with words. Allowing silence for 2–3 seconds is better than inserting an "uh". Try pausing after one of your strongest sentences to look your audience right in the eye and gauge their reaction.

5. Go early and make plenty of eye contact before the meeting. Interact with audience members. Talk with them and learn of their current interests and concerns. Those who spoke with you before the program will likely be showing you the most attentive faces when it is your turn to speak.

6. Start slow. Keep your opening sentence short and easy to say. These two things give the audience time to warm up to you. Adjust to them at the same time by establishing eye contact.

7. Smile with your eyes. Think what a difference a smile can make in a voice projected over the phone. Likewise, projecting the thought of a smile in your eye can work for you too. Practice this in the mirror to appreciate the subtle but positive difference it makes.

8. Know your first sentence cold. For example: Have you ever heard a speaker say, "Good morning. My name is…" as he looks down to read his name? Knowing your first line enables you to begin your speech with solid eye contact.

9. Counterbalance any negative thoughts by telling yourself a positive thought just before you begin speaking. I once had a dentist tell me he repeated the word "humility" to himself before starting his weekly staff meeting. He said it helped him relax so much in front of groups that he tried imagining the word was on his forehead each time he greeted a patient. Silly? Yes, but the result was warm eye contact — and better communication — with his staff and patients.

10. The "scoop 'n speak" technique. If you must read a prepared script, then this technique is definitely worth considering. As a viewer, you have seen it used in high-level addresses by politicians, heads of state, and corporate presidents at annual meetings.

Prepare your notes in large fonts, but not entirely in capital letters (they really are difficult to read). Double-space the entire text. Next, practice scooping up a tightly written line with your eyes, looking up and saying what you've just read. The goal is always to be looking toward the audience and making contact while your mouth is moving.

During the learning curve, clients often tell me how "weird" this feels. It does feel unnatural at first, but it looks and sounds good to the audience. With practice, and after critiquing your video performance, you'll soon see the usefulness of this technique. Your audience will appreciate the added eye contact, too.

Unfortunately, there is a lot of bad advice out there when it comes to eye contact. Several books on public speaking suggest that if you have trouble looking at people, you should try staring just over the top of their heads, or focusing on a spot on the back wall. The smaller the audience, the more disturbing this becomes. Far too often, presenters end up ignoring the audience and talking to the projection screen! Don't fool yourself: if you're not really making eye contact with the audience, they will know the difference.

Carl, a knowledgeable CPA, had the habit of looking directly at the stomachs of people in the audience as he spoke. He was quite comfortable with his technique, though he knew he wasn't making the best impression. During a class, I asked him if I could make a training adjustment as he spoke. We agreed that every time I snapped my fingers, he would look up. Carl began speaking and staring into the mid-section of a lady on the front row. After a few seconds, I snapped my fingers. As instructed, Carl looked up, but the pressure of trying to make eye contact with the audience caused his eyes to glaze over. He was still talking, but seemed in a trance.

Fortunately, after another minute of feeling safe and not being reprimanded; Carl's eyes cleared for the first time, and he finally met the eyes of the audience members. Unsolicited applause from the class helped cement this new behavior.

Lack of eye contact was apparently all that was preventing Carl's leadership qualities from shining through. A few weeks later, after continuing to practice his newfound skills, he called to tell me that he had been promoted to accounting department manager.

Three ways to outsmart yourself

These gimmicks may work for you, but not for your audience:

- **Picking one or two people in the audience and talking mostly to them.** It's okay to start this way, if it's the only way you can settle down, but within seconds you need to cover more territory. If you keep talking to a select few, you will alienate everyone else in the room and make the targeted person wish you had more friends.
- **Looking at a spot halfway down the center aisle and talking to it.** Lawyers sometimes do this as they walk around courtrooms. To me, it looks like the speaker is looking for roaches. (Very distracting.)

- **Keeping your eyes moving at all times.** This is like keeping a lit match in motion: nothing will take fire until you hold it still. By the same token, no one in your audience will get fired up until your eyes pause and connect.

To recap: without solid eye contact, you'll never earn the trust of your audience. It takes practice to do this with a sea of people, but can you remember how hard it was to keep your eyes on the road and your car's gauges when you first were learning to drive? It gets easier over time.

Eventually, you will get used to the intimacy of really looking into your audience's eyes, and the positive feedback they give you will reward your efforts. Trying will bring success. There is no other way.

To make oneself understood to people, one must first speak to their eyes. – Napoleon

Additional insights

- Have a friend watch you as you speak and give you feedback afterward. Ask him or her if you spoke to the whole audience or if you had a tendency to favor one side or to look mostly at people in the front row. Normally, eye contact should be maintained for two to three seconds before shifting your attention somewhere else.
- Never address your notes, flipcharts, or dry erase boards. They're poor listeners, and they *never* applaud!
- If direct contact is difficult, try fooling yourself by looking into one eye of a listener. Then as you feel more comfortable, look at both eyes. This sounds silly, but I've seen it help presenters overcome avoidance problems.
- When an audience is so large that it's impossible to look everyone in the eye, try looking into *areas* to establish connection.

- We are almost always attracted to those who are attracted to us. Why? Could be several reasons, but probably the main reason is when another person pays attention to us, it makes us feel good about ourselves. It gives us a slight ego boost and increases our sense of self-worth.

NINE

ENERGY

To _keep_ an audience listening, you must project energy.

In an operating room, cries of "We're losing him! We're losing him!" could mean death if unheeded. Still, in meetings how many times have we unconsciously said to ourselves, "You're losing me. I can't look at another overhead," or "I can't listen anymore. I'm tuning out now. Bye." Hospital patients are not responsible for monitoring their vital signs, but speakers are responsible for managing their own energy level if they want to hold their listeners' interest.

It's like pouring water into a large sponge. The sponge retains most of the flow at first, but as we continue to pour more water, it becomes saturated until eventually it can hold nothing more. (For wringing techniques, see Chapter 15: Variety.)

Don't mistake your listeners' _initial interest_ as a guarantee of continued interest. An audience's initial interest in your presentation is a gift, but their continued interest is a reward, and it must be earned.

Energy is what fills the space between people.

Even a professionally written speech can lose listeners if there's insufficient energy behind the words. No wonder we enjoy watching dramatic plays and movies where actors remind us of how humans feel and express varied emotions. People will stand in line, in the rain, to watch a movie, but rarely to hear a lecturer, unless it's an exciting speaker.

Energy connects things — particularly the distance between performer and audience. Even if you are knowledgeable in a given subject, if you *read* your speech from your notes or from PowerPoint slides, people will find it difficult to listen. It's like listening to an answering machine; if the message takes longer than a minute to hear, you'll likely hit the *bypass* button or just disconnect. Why? It's painful to listen at length to something or someone when we don't feel connected. (See Chapter 12: Audience Expectations.)

There are rare times when words don't require energy to really be heard — for example, when the company president is announcing the names of people getting raises or being laid off, or when a jury is returning its verdict.

But, all too often presenters are out of touch with their level of energy projection. Usually, they place too much importance on the weight of their bullet points and too little on the amount of gunpowder they need to penetrate the consciousness of their listeners.

Generally, audiences want to laugh, rally behind a cause, listen to stories, enjoy themselves — and feel something.
– Roger Ailes

Expressed energy and energy reserved

Singing has a great deal to do with energy, both expressed and reserved. The explosive projection of opera singer Luciano Pavarotti is an obvious example of energy expressed. But the quiet, magnetic attraction of an assertive person like speaker and author Deepak Chopra — with his latent reserves of strength and presence — has an equally powerful effect. The confidence you derive from proper preparation and knowledge of your subject will work silently and invisibly to your advantage.

Mahatma Gandhi was another leader who, though slight of build, projected enormous powers of resistance and influence. His quiet confidence came from several elements: a prepared mind, a clear-cut objective, and a commitment to a cause bigger than himself.

Is it my voice?

Occasionally, people call our office wanting help in projecting their voices. If they have no physical impairment, we can help them, because the voice is not usually the real problem. If you were to slap this person and steal their youngest offspring, they would most likely raise their voice and yell at you. The habit of not projecting their voice comes from a natural hesitancy and learned tendency to avoid pain.

Somewhere in the past these people experienced so much discomfort because of someone else's loud voice that they became conditioned not to raise their own. The solution is simple, but takes training. And, similar to taking antibiotics, a one-day dose won't do much good. In fact, the "patient" will probably get worse unless he or she takes the full prescription.

I have found that if my students have the chance to raise their voices in a safe training environment, once a week for four to six weeks, the experience can profoundly affect their speaking confidence.

In fact, most people who speak timidly are held back not from their physical inability to speak up, but from fear. Under the right circumstances, their inhibitions can disappear amazingly fast. (Who hasn't been shocked by at least one corporate mouse who roared at a company party after indulging in too much eggnog? The false courage he or she gained from the alcohol destroyed his or her fear, allowing for a remarkable voice projection.) (See Chapter 22: Voice.)

Energy blocks

The biggest energy obstacle is fear — fear of imperfection. Whether we're playing a musical instrument or answering questions in a crucial interview, we can block our natural power by insisting on a perfect performance. Going for a "10" when hard work has made you a "9" is a worthy goal. If you're stuck at "3," however, and can accept nothing less than a perfect "10," you'll never grow, and you'll waste energy in self-censure that could have been used to create a positive outcome.

Anything worth doing is worth doing badly. For it is in trying that we learn how to do things well.
– Jana Stanfield

Our power is best spent practicing and projecting our best self, the person we are right now. Trying to act perfect causes inward focus instead of outward attention to listeners. A speaker who focuses on governing his words, gestures, and "uhs" will sound stilted and unnatural.

The greatest mistake you can make in life is to be continually fearing you will make one.
– Elbert Hubbard

10 ways to raise your energy level:

1. **Shift concerns** about your own well being to the vitality of your performance. If you're focused on the "big you," you hold back energy that should infuse your delivery.

2. **Before speaking,** imagine you hear bugles blowing and drums beating — calling you to rise to the occasion! If you don't sense the significance of what you are saying, others won't pay much attention, either. Take responsibility for being able to tap your energy whenever you need it. If what you are saying is important, you have a responsibility to find the energy to connect with the group. *If the trumpet makes an uncertain sound, who shall prepare himself for battle?* I Corinthians 14:8

3. **Prepare a *simple* outline** to serve as the foundation for your presentation the way a railroad track serves as a base for the engineer, allowing him to focus on building up steam and power.

4. **Pause and find your breath** within the hour before you speak. Judge how well you are breathing. When you inhale, does your stomach expand or contract? If you're taking full breaths, it should expand. Practice breathing slowly and comfortably, filling your entire diaphragm (not just the upper portion of your lungs) with air. Don't force it. Concentrate on your breath until you can easily take a complete, full breath. Imagine blowing through a narrow straw as you exhale slowly through your mouth.

5. **Get extra rest.** Give yourself the amount of rest you know you need to feel energized. This may require excusing yourself early from a dinner engagement the night before, or taking an earlier flight to your destination in order to make time to relax.

6. **Exercise.** If you can't do physical calisthenics ahead of time, try brisk walking. Carry a sheet of paper in your hand and

walk toward someone's office at the far end of the building and back.

7. **Don't sit** right next to the podium or speaking area. The short walk from your chair at the end of the table can help get your blood flowing.

8. **Keep your hands out of your pockets** and unclasped. Griping your wrist or anything else uses energy.

9. **Double the size** of your gestures. Unless you're talking one-on-one and in someone's face, it's hard to use a gesture that is too big. Remember: Space equals power.

10. **Walk briskly** to the front of the room. Remember how much you wanted to share your answer with the class when you were six? Prepare well — then act and move with confidence. You communicate your energy (interest level) long before you say a word.

Manage excess energy.

Avoiding nervous movements is a matter of managing energy. For example, if you hold the lectern with a two-handed death grip and rock it side-to-side like you're trying to move a clothes dryer, you will dilute your message. Let go and redirect all that nervous energy into more enthusiasm and sincere interest in what you say. Released from nervous tension, your spirit will flow. The result will be better vocal emphasis and larger, action-oriented gestures. People will naturally pay more attention to you because you are trying harder to reach them.

You don't have to shout to speak with energy. Intensity can be expressed with a whisper. Whatever your style, it must come across to listeners as power. The weight of your words or color hue of your Power Point slides is rarely enough.

Using energy is simply speaking with uninhibited conviction. It will help keep your audience listening, so they don't finish listening before you finish speaking.

Fearless and Persuasive Speaking

A man can be short and dumpy and bald but if he has fire,
women will like him.
– Mae West

Additional insights

- If you sound boring, the audience will have to use more of their energy — if they choose to listen.
- The bigger the audience, the bigger the possibility of creating an energy-charged environment — but you must prime them with your energy first.
- Be a giver of energy, not a blocker.
- Don't delay your enthusiasm, by waiting to see if they like you first.
- Show people that you are alive today! Focused, purposeful and energetic people attract others!
- Ask someone to listen to your talk and note the times they "feel" something from you.
- Take responsibility for raising your overall energy. No one knows how to make this happen better than you.

TEN

INVOLVEMENT

Talk less — involve more

If you grew up hearing lectures from teachers, parents, or preachers, then the idea of involving an audience might sound foreign to you, because most speakers lecture rather than involve their audience.

> *He is not only dull himself, but the cause of dullness in others.*
> – Boswell's *Life of Samuel Johnson* (Johnson's parody of
> Shakespeare's Henry IV, (Part II, I.ii.7)

But think about the best teachers you ever had. What did you like about them? What was it like being in their classroom? Chances are, these special leaders didn't bore you with long monologues, but engaged you with the subject at hand.

How? Well, you could say they had a knack or that they enjoyed their subjects so much that people just naturally got more interested. All very true, perhaps, but they also knew this secret: people learn more when they are involved in the learning process than when they are fed information.

The right attitude

Whether the purpose of your speech is increased sales, better grades or productivity, or a more exciting vacation, the first ingredient is desire. You must communicate to the audience that you welcome their participation. Are you convinced that more good could come from a group effort? Are you willing to share the spotlight?

Every Monday morning, Roger Jones (the name is changed to protect the guilty), an operations manager for a chain of grocery stores, meets with his nine area managers. Each week the format is predictably the same: Roger talks for almost two hours, and then asks if there are any quick questions. Rarely does anyone postpone the opportunity for adjournment by asking a question! Believing his troops have been motivated and that communication has occurred, Roger dismisses the groggy group, expecting them to go forth and inspire others. Sound familiar?

Better to have one person working with you than three people working for you. – Dwight D. Eisenhower

How could Roger improve his meetings, engage the managers, and demonstrate more effective leadership? One idea might be to have two different managers a week make a presentation to the group — by assigning them five-to-seven minutes each on a topic they know well. For example, one could present a report on how a 10% cost reduction or sales increase was achieved during the last quarter.

Another could inform the group on the finer points of implementing a new accounting package, lead a discussion on customer service, or demonstrate how to build an eye-catching display. (If you are in a similar situation, think about spearheading such a project yourself. It could give you more experience speaking on a subject you know well. Who knows, even the "Roger" in your organization might welcome the participation.)

Three cornerstones to foster involvement:

1. **Care** – You must care more about the group's achievement than about personal gratification. If people are attentive or even appreciative but don't retain your information, try something different.

2. **Share** – You should share the process, not dominate it. This means believing in synergy (the sum of the parts is greater than the whole). Allow others to add to the sum of the meeting. Shared information adds up. For example, if you give me a dollar and I give you a dollar, we both would still have a dollar. But if you give me an idea and I give you an idea, we would each have two ideas.

3. **Respect** – Be genuinely interested in the audience as people. Use examples and analogies tailored to them. Offering respect to others is not only being polite: it's communicating to others on an adult-to-adult level, being careful not to slip into the parent-speaking-to-child style. It's characterized by small differences like asking them to turn to the next page instead of ordering them to do it. Or, occasionally asking, "What is your opinion?" versus always telling them the answer. Whether or not they have a better answer, their opinions count.

Ken Bradford

The right techniques

Consider the following 20 proven methods for involving your listeners in the communication process:

1. Offer sincere praise. Point out the positive aspects of this particular group and share your observations with them. Be sure you are sharing a specific reason for your praise, though, or it could sound like insincere flattery. Imagine the audience is always silently challenging your praise with the question "Why?" If you aren't prepared to answer the question honestly and specifically, then do more research on the group's background attributes.

The late Mary Kay Ash of the Mary Kay cosmetics company was a master at involvement. For example, here is how she once opened a large company meeting: "I know that all of you have traveled some distance to be here today. Some of you have even journeyed for days. But I want you to know that no one has really gone anywhere. You are all right where you have always been ... here ... right next to my heart." After 14 minutes of standing and applauding, audience members finally let her continue speaking. She was sincere. She had done her homework. So can you.

The applause of a single human being is of great consequence.
– Samuel Johnson

Whatever gets rewarded grows. You have the ability to help elevate good ideas to the level of great ideas. You can also offer positive reinforcement if you notice some willing participation during the meeting or comment on the participation you noticed during the last meeting, or praise the level of involvement shown by the participants who organized the meeting. Again, just make sure you are absolutely sincere.

Fearless and Persuasive Speaking

Praise is a form of encouragement. Truett Cathy, founder of the Chick Fil-A Restaurants, also believes in the power of giving people positive feedback. He says that his number one responsibility at work is giving encouragement to employees. How does he know who needs encouragement? Mr. Cathy says, "If they are breathing, they need encouragement."

2. **Ask questions.** If you don't get much response, consider that your question may not be clear or the answer may be too obvious. Remember to pause five to seven seconds after asking a question to give people time to think. Two good questions to ask after introducing the topic are "What's your opinion?" and "Here's an example, what are some more?" The latter one encourages people to speak from their own experiences. As you are preparing your talk, look for places where a good question will advance the agenda as well as audience understanding.

There are very few people who don't become more interesting when they stop speaking.
– Mary Lowry

3. **Share responsibility and authority.** Allow someone from the group to present a segment of the next meeting. Help them be successful by giving them ample time to prepare. Suggest they cover three main points and tell them the time frame you expect. (Keep it short and simple at first, maybe five minutes.) The key is to prepare the presenter, hear his or her comments before the group does, and give sincere praise. When others see how well the presenter was treated, they will be more apt to get involved next time. People usually support what they help create.

4. **Use inclusive language.** For example: "You know." "You've all experienced similar situations." "Make sense?" "As you

can see." "Let's look at..." "Important?" "What's next?" Exclusive language sounds like "I want you to..." or "I know what I'm talking about..."or "Go do it" as opposed to "Let's go."

5. **Use recursive examples.** Recursive is a word of Latin origin for recur or return to. In other words, go back to get the real thing to explain the thing. If, for example, you're talking about a particular modem, or a motherboard, or your mother's pizza, bring the example (or prop) with you to the meeting. If you're talking about a result, or a problem, or the competition's features, get a tangible representation of it. Bring a book about it, and use it to show what you mean. A prop is three-dimensional, which is almost always more interesting for the audience than just talking about the subject or trying to describe it by using a slide.

6. **Mention the names of a few of your listeners.** Remember how you used to sit up straighter when the teacher called your name? I'm not suggesting you correct audience members, but it's human nature to listen more closely when your own name is being mentioned. By asking questions, acknowledging contributions, and recognizing successful audience members by name, you will retain your listeners' attention.

7. **Survey the audience and find common ground.** Find out all you can about your listeners' interest in your subject. If they have minimal exposure to or interest in your topic, discern how your message can benefit them by using your expertise in a given topic to build a bridge connecting your experiences with theirs. If you haven't surveyed the group before the meeting starts, you might poll them at the beginning of the meeting. The more you know about what's important to the people listening, the better you can prioritize your points.

8. **Enumerate.** Numbering your points has three benefits. First, it signals a finite body of information that audiences can focus on. Second, it helps you stay on track. Third, if you get off-track, your listeners can and will likely point this out to you.

9. **Ask for physical action.** Religious leaders have used this for centuries (responsive reading, kneeling, shaking hands with other worshippers, and coming forward to the altar). Retail clothing salespeople know to ask, "Would you like to try it on?" Physical action encourages mental willingness. One method is to have people talk to someone they did not know well before the meeting began.

10. **Think, write, and share.** Did you ever ask a group a question and receive little or no response? It could be that they needed more time to formulate an answer. The Think, Write, and Share formula can help. Ask everyone to think for a moment before responding. Next, ask them to write down a couple of their responses. Then ask them to reiterate their answers with a partner in the audience. Finally, ask them to share their responses (or their partner's response) with the group.

11. **Use a demonstration.** Demonstrations are twice as effective when an audience member is asked to come forward and help. Avoid using the word "volunteer." (Rumor has it that "volunteer" is another name for "victim.")

12. **The Sweep Technique.** Casually begin your talk on the way up to the front. When your talk is initiated from behind the audience, you will grab their attention even more. (Remember how much neck-twisting attention we give to a bride's entrance.)

13. **Divide and conquer.** Have everyone count off. If you want to end up with four groups, count off: 1, 2, 3, 4, 1, 2, 3, 4, etc. Then, have people move to their new group without moving their chairs. When we must adapt to a new situation, we are more alert and energized. This also helps with the problem of people sitting only with people they know.

    Random pairing is a quick way to mix and engage people. If you want to use triads, count off in three's or A, B, Cs and let two people role-play the topic and the third act as the coach, offering helpful feedback and suggestions for improvement after the exercise is over. Then A, B, and C change roles and repeat the exercise. In a short time, everyone in the group will have had a chance to send, receive, and observe the topic. The more ways we experience a subject, the deeper our understanding.

14. **Establish goals.** Recently, I divided my class into two groups. I asked the first half to step out into the hallway to work on a project. Once outside, and out of hearing range from the students in the classroom, I asked if they could write down fifty qualities of a leader in three minutes. Stepping back into the classroom, I asked the other half to write down the qualities of a leader. After three minutes, the group in the classroom had 23 items. The hallway group had 50. Establishing a measurable goal and a time boundary creates a challenge, and who doesn't enjoy an occasional challenge?

15. **Cumulative strengths.** Start by appointing someone to serve as mathematician. One at a time, ask each person on the front row, "How long have you been in this industry?" Have the mathematician keep score and get a cumulative total. To get a rough tally, multiply the years of experience on the front row by the total number of rows. Then you could say something like "With over a century of experience right here in this room today, I know you will have a lot to share on this subject."

16. **Trade a prize for an answer.** I was in the audience the other day when a speaker announced that he had three questions for us. When someone answered the first one, he surprised everyone by giving the responder a cassette tape on the subject. With a prize at stake, you can bet we were twice as motivated to answer the next two questions!

17. **Establish a dialogue versus a monologue atmosphere.** More people will respond if they feel it's okay to interact with you, but you have to invite them. Dialogue begins with you asking the audience good questions. It increases or decreases depending on how you treat the first few to respond. (Remember the three elements of attitude mentioned earlier in this chapter? Care, share, and respect.) Show grateful appreciation for all sincere responses. After all, you did ask.

18. **Plant the seed.** Ask participants to think about your topic prior to the meeting. Let them know you welcome their ideas. Unless you are trying to creep up and surprise them, remind them of the topic again the day before the meeting to cultivate thinking. Sometimes, this gives people enough time to bring great examples or data with them to your meeting.

19. **Have the audience find something.** Here are three ideas to get you started. I'm sure you will be able to think of additional scenarios appropriate to your topic.

    A) Show how to do something. For example, a bank manager could show how to transfer funds electronically to another bank, and then say, "There are three mistakes in this example. Who sees the first one?" Often, it's easier asking people to criticize and judge something than asking them to find the positive.

B) Compose a list of abbreviations relevant to your topic and the audience's experience. For example, at a financial planners meeting, the speaker provided a list of twenty-five abbreviations such as CPA, CMA, CFP, CLU, FIFO, GAAP, FDIC, SIPC, etc. The assignment was to spell-out the words represented by the acronyms. We were seated in tables of six, so each group around a table worked as a team. The first table with all the answers sent a representative running to the front table to claim a prize. I had never met anyone at my table before, but within ten seconds, we were united and involved.
C) Before the meeting begins, tape a $20 bill to the underside of a chair. As you end the program, have everyone stand and then look on the bottom side of their chairs for something. After one person finds the money announce, "That demonstrates my last point. Nothing of value ever happens until we get off our rears!"

20. **Leave the room.** Trusting people with responsibility helps them grow. First provide direction. Then make sure that participants understand the objective. You might even use a staged excuse to leave the room, so it can be their idea to take over. Avoid saying, "I'll be back to check up on you later." Try saying something like, "Do you think it's possible as a group to come up with the answers on your own, while I take care of something?"

Those who implement the plans must help make the plans.
– Patrick Haggerty, past chairman,
Texas Instruments

When we're willing to share the speaking process with people we respect, we may give up a little control, but we gain respect as leaders.

Additional insights

- Information becomes at least three times more memorable when audiences are allowed to participate.
- Physical involvement works even better if introduced early on.
- When you want a show of hands in response to a question you are asking, raise your hand as you introduce the question. This provides a signal for how to respond.
- Involvement is often easier when audience members are sitting close together, but not close enough to cause discomfort.
- If you always have too many empty chairs, especially on the front row, remove them before the meeting starts.

Tell me and I'll forget. Show me and I'll remember. Involve me and I'll understand. – Confucius

ELEVEN

VISUALS

Manage the visual image, starting with your own.

L eading a meeting — even just describing anything to a group requires your presence — up front. This means more than just being in the room and jockeying a projector. Visual aids are just that — aids, not the whole show. As such, they should support what you are saying without overpowering the point of your message.

What's the most important visual? You, of course, because people want to connect with real, live folks, not machines.

When making any presentation, understand that first impressions of you and your subject start very early, even before you open your mouth. The minute a group recognizes you as the next speaker, they begin evaluating you. They may pass judgment as soon as you walk into the room, when you first meet them in the hallway, or even in the parking lot.

So make sure that before every presentation, you stop by the restroom first to make sure your tie is straight, pocket flaps are out, slip isn't showing, shoes are tied, belt fastened, etc. Finish dressing *before* you're introduced or prior to starting the meeting. When you appear before an audience, avoid leaning against the wall or on the corner of the table. Let your arms swing naturally as you walk. Put your energy into good posture. Your posture is the most revealing message you are sending. And please don't wait until you are ready to speak before looking at the audience. They like attention. Acknowledge their presence with your eyes and face as soon as possible.

Your attitude starts the ball rolling and your feet moving. Walk like you're happy — not condemned — to be there. Step up to home plate with energy. Let it show in your walk — erect, but relaxed. Walk slightly faster than usual. Move with the determination of one who knows the answer, has a purpose and can't wait to tell everyone. You'll look like a leader and move like one if your attitude is right. Essentially, you must look confident to be taken as competent.

Everyone is a winner on paper.
It is in the flesh that the difference stands out.

Why use visual aids?

As a teen I proudly worked at my first real job, as a french-fry cook at a hamburger joint. A large mirror hung just over the cooking vat where fries sputtered and sent grease projectiles into the air. Whenever the manager walked by, he would remind me to keep the mirror clean. I thought that the whole idea of a having a mirror so close to boiling grease was pretty idiotic and that it was doubly idiotic to keep cleaning it.

One day I asked again why I constantly had to wipe down the mirror. Instead of answering me directly, he just said, "Bend down and look into that mirror! Now, tell me what you see." I said, "I see the front window where customers stand and place their orders." "So, what do you think they see as they're standing there?" he asked. "French fries," I replied. "Ken, don't ever forget — people buy what they can see. Now clean your mirror." I still hated cleaning that mirror, but it finally made sense.

Think about what it is you want to drive home to your audience, and find a way to make that real for them. They will listen more attentively when they can see what you're talking about. Everyone in attendance may not be from Missouri, but you can pretend they're from the "Show Me State" as you ask yourself what points can be made clearer and stronger using a visual aid.

Any subject can be made more interesting with some type of visual aid. Under the right circumstances, you might use the following: props, flipcharts, dry-erase boards, permanent posters, enlarged photos, slides, film clips, or overhead projectors.

Which aids and when?

Function dictates what to use when. For variety, almost any visual aid that's different from the last one you've used is fine. But for larger groups, you'll need a little extra help. A good rule of thumb to remember is that the larger the group, the larger the visual required. A flipchart illustration is great, but if the person in the back row can't see it, you'll need something larger like a slide projector, very big prop, multiple visuals circulated throughout the audience, or multiple props that can be distributed randomly to the audience. A good example is the small toy footballs or basketballs you see being tossed around a large crowd before a sporting event.

Prop up your talk with props.

Props add believability to your message, and believability is everything. If your listeners don't believe you, they'll stop listening. A salesman I was working with wanted to convince his customers (grocery store managers) to buy a plastic fork and spoon line, but he was receiving a lot of objections over the fact that the product contained benzene, a chemical used for dyeing and cleaning. The managers refused to carry his line. The following week he had to give the same presentation to an identical group of managers. He explained to me that benzene at certain higher levels could be poisonous, but that at lower levels, it was widely used to make several food products like pretzels.

So, I suggested he use a prop, a bag of pretzels. He put a lunch-box size bag of pretzels on each chair, about forty packages total, and scheduled the meeting just prior to lunch. Sure enough, the objection over benzene was raised again by one the audience members. This time, he told the audience that the level of benzene used to manufacture his products was no higher than that commonly used to make pretzels like the ones they were snacking on. The prop worked. The managers were convinced and the salesman got a huge order.

Props as substitutes for notes

Remembering what comes next with note cards or sheets of paper is sometimes hard, but it's a lot easier if you have a physical object — a prop — staring you in the face. Props can be transitions to the next idea you want to express. They silently prompt you to move ahead. Also, when you finish using them, the audience feels a sense of accomplishment and order. Props aren't a substitute for all notes, but they might replace some of them.

Props have rules

Vanna White, co-host of the television game show *Wheel of Fortune,* understands the rules for using props. First, you don't turn over your cards, or whatever objects you're going to show, until you're ready to make your point. The timing of its exposure should be in sync with your verbal message, not before or afterward. Too often, presenters hold up their prop before they are ready to make their point with it. The audience has already seen it and started asking themselves questions about it. Second, hold the prop high enough to be seen by everyone, including the people in the back row or in the periphery. Vanna knows how to stand to the side of the letter she is turning, and remain square-shouldered to the audience. Third, don't talk to the prop. You won't get a response and the audience will feel abandoned. Vanna sees the letter, turns it, and smiles at the viewers, not the prop. Fourth, once people have had a good look at the prop and you've made your point, put it away. If you have more to say, you don't want your verbal message to compete with the visual you just used.

The mind flows where the eye goes. – Unknown

Prove your expertise with a flipchart

Live animals always attract attention on television talk shows, but live animals might be harmful to your listeners. A live presentation on a flipchart is a nice substitute for an unruly beast. You can introduce the flipchart at any time during your presentation and easily refer back to it to reinforce a previous point. Flipchart illustrations look unplanned, not canned like a lot of slide-show illustrations.

They also add a personal touch to your presentation by allowing you to show your own depth of understanding or familiarity with the topic. Anyone can have a slide built with lots of carefully planned facts attached, but if you can draw your own illustration or write your points out from memory onto a sheet of flipchart paper in front of a live audience, you look more like an expert. Don't worry if you are not Rembrandt. Just keep your writing and illustrations very simple and large.

Ken Bradford

A lesson from the Great Communicator

President Ronald Reagan used signs to explain the principle of supply and demand on national television. He was the first president to use a sign card on television. The next day, the news media proclaimed him the Great Communicator. Why? The signs followed the flow of his spoken message with very little deviation. Rather than cutting to an off-stage illustration or a projection screen behind him, he chose a sign. He wanted to stay close to the viewer and let his spoken message be reinforced with a visual image, held right in his hand, which is where he held us, too.

Permanent signs add authority to any message. Consider having your most vital piece of information printed on a permanent plastic sign, (like a real estate agent would use) which you can use repeatedly. Its permanent look will add credence to your presentation and help you remember an important message.

Slides: Advantages

Organizing your thoughts by preparing a slide presentation is one way to start preparing a talk. This mechanical process forces you to think about one cell at a time and how your ideas will unfold. Slides can be projected on a screen, which is adjustable to the size of most any group. Everyone can see a large screen or multiple media screens. To stress the details, you can easily duplicate your storyboard on the handouts.

Slides: Disadvantages

First, slides are not personable. They are not you. Don't remove yourself from the presentation by relying on electronic panels to do your job for you. No matter how clever or colorful, they remain inanimate objects. By starting in the dark and standing to the side, you are already deserting the throne.

Second, there is a tendency to build a slide presentation based on the amount of time allotted for presenting. This approach can create overkill: too many slides, too little focus on the needs of the audience and the essence of your message.

Be sensitive to the listener's capacity to absorb information. Don't be guilty of "death by bullets." Too often speakers mistake the initial receptiveness of a fresh audience as a permanent willingness to listen. Having this misperception is like interpreting a neighbor's willingness to loan you a cup of sugar as a signal that they want to cook your dinner. Use as few slides as possible to convey key messages. If necessary, use any extra time for audience discussion.

The third disadvantage of using an all-slide program is the tendency of the presenter to read the information to the audience as they are also attempting to read the slide. Reading speed varies for all of us, and doing two things at once is bothersome. Your audience is being forced to ignore your voice, ignore the visual aid, or ignore you and the slide and think about something totally different. This is similar to talking to a person while they're trying to read the newspaper.

Speaking while the audience is trying to read a slide with bullet points divides their attention. They cannot read and listen at the same time. Think how difficult it would be to try to read this chapter while I'm talking to you! The solution is to boil down the words on slides to as few as possible, so the audience can understand your points quickly and return its focus to you. Jimmy Caberera makes a living presenting motivational talks to teen-age audiences, and he knows how to boil down his ideas. Despite the generation gap, he is very influential with young audiences. To convey the importance of getting an education, he uses a few slides. On one of them, which appears only for seconds, is the word STAY, in bold red letters on a black background. The message is simple, but the impact is profound.

I once worked with a public relations company that coached executives who made crucial I.P.O. (initial public offering) presentations to investment bankers. After weighing all the issues and facts presented by company executives, the investment bankers set the initial price of the company's stock. A stock price slightly higher or lower could mean millions to a new firm.

During the practice session with executives, the corporate controller was presenting data when the public relations consultant abruptly interrupted, saying, "Quit reading the @#$*# slides to us! Your job is to tell us what they mean!" The result was a much more interesting presentation, because the controller began to share his insights from thirty-four years of experience.

Don't let slides lead your thoughts, by clicking on one and then talking about it before going on to the next. Give variety to your message by sometimes making a point and then showing the slide that reinforces it. Or, pause to let people read a simple slide, and then ask them what's important about it. Put yourself in the shoes of the audience members. You don't want to be machined-gunned by a slide projector and a trigger-happy projectionist.

Keep yourself in the presentation. If you use a projection screen, keep it up front, but put it off to the side. When the screen is in the center, the screen is the focal point. When you are in the center, you are the focal point.

Visuals are for making your message bigger, more powerful, and more believable. They must be relevant and are more interesting if they are novel. Don't limit your presentation to just slides. Explore your options first, then use the best visual to fit the circumstance.

For every step forward in electronic communications we've taken two steps back in humanity. People know how to use a computer and fax, but have forgotten how to connect with one another.
– Letitia Baldridge

Additional insights

- To a huge extent, you are the message as well as the messenger.
- Visuals break up the facts into separate, understandable packages.
- Create a one-page cheat sheet that lists the slide number and a one or two-word description of what is on the slide. This enables you to type in the number of the slide and hit return to bring it up, accelerating the search for your next destination and allowing more flexibility for extemporaneous changes in order. This is also very helpful when a one-hour presentation must be cut in half at the last minute.
- More is often less. If you can say the same thing with half the words, do so.
- Give all visuals the "back row" test. Can people in the last row easily read the text?
- Position screens at an angle behind you so that your body never blocks the audience's view.
- If you must darken the room so the audience can see the screen, try to get an extra source of light on you.
- Beware of monotonous patterns like a company a logo or motto appearing on every slide.

TWELVE

AUDIENCE EXPECTATIONS

If you don't know them, they may not want to know you.

Groucho Marx once told a fledgling comedian who was about to step onto stage, "Don't worry. They don't expect much." Thinking an audience expects little of you is one sure way to fall on your face. The truth is: audiences expect a lot. They have a checklist. Some items are conscious, but many are unconscious. Paying attention to them before you start could save you time and regret later.

The audience expects you to be:

___ **Prepared**. Early on listeners ask themselves, "Is my time being spent in a meaningful manner?" Add to their knowledge, but don't waste their time. They would rather waste money than time. You never hear anyone on his deathbed asking for more money.

___**In the moment**. Usually within seconds, the audience realizes if you are focused on talking with them or focused on your text and talking at them. You may be physically present, but still hiding inside yourself or behind notes or a lectern. Audiences want the leader to display a sense of caring and the appropriate feeling for the occasion (for example, a sense of humility when receiving an award). We see sports figures sometimes caught off guard and mocking the defeated team, which often results in a positive feeling toward the loser and disgust for the victor.

At a charity event the other evening a local television anchorperson served as master of ceremonies. Looking straight ahead as if still speaking into a television camera, she carefully read to a live audience for 20 minutes. It's an odd feeling to be in the same room as the speaker, but left feeling like it wouldn't have mattered if we had melted into a drain opening. If you have written a speech to simply be read, you are already denying half the needs of the audience.

A paper that is read is like a kiss on the telephone
– pleasant but not the real thing. – Albert Sabin

___**Making eye contact.** Audiences want to be noticed. (See Chapter 8: Eye Contact.)

The speaker's eye: the most elusive organ that
Nature ever created. – Stanley Baldwin

___**Committed to your message.** Outstanding presenters give their all. Lesser speakers do what they can to get by. There's a big difference between contributing and being fully committed. For example: When a chicken contributes to breakfast, it gives eggs, but when a hog contributes, he fully commits.

___**Interested in the subject.** (See Chapter 6: Countenance) You're interesting in proportion to your involvement in the subject. It is hard to get others interested in your subject if you're not. Offer more facts than opinions, but make sure that your stories and examples always include a relevant point.

___ **Sharing your viewpoint.** Instead of only giving information that anyone could find in a library, give your opinion on the matter. If they didn't want it, they would have asked someone else to speak.

___ **Inspired.** Your message should move you enough from the inside that you manifest an outward physical expression. Even if you are apprehensive, if the message inside you is bigger than the thoughts about yourself, you will not appear nervous. The rescuer running into the burning childcare center doesn't worry about voice inflection or whether his shoes are polished; he is message and audience-focused, not self-focused.

___ **Timely.** Start on time, and definitely end on time. Whether the audience members are punctual or not, they will expect you to respect their time.

___ **Aware of who they are.** The audience's unspoken feeling should be, "You know who we are. You care enough to see us as individuals, not just a crowd. You identified with my concerns." If you want people to be interested in you, show an interest in them right away. Create a short survey. Take a poll. Call or walk around to visit with individuals who will be in the audience later. Understand how they feel on your topic. What do they need, want, fear, have a sense of pride about? What are they tired of? What do they want more or less of?

The audience gives you everything you need. They tell you. There is no director who can direct you like an audience.
– Fanny Brice

___ **Organized**. Don't bother telling them you're not prepared — if you're not, they'll know. Think the subject through logically and you will discover how to keep things simple. Your value to the audience is calculated according to how much you help them. Don't wander down too many rabbit trails that don't relate to the topic.

___ **Knowledgeable**. Through first-hand experience, formal education, or extra study, you have earned the right to talk on the subject. As much as possible, make your subject relate to the audience's own personal interest.

___ **Clear**. You speak without leaving your audience with more questions than when you began. Your important points are well thought out and easy to interpret.

*If the speaker won't boil it down, the audience must
sweat it out.* – Raymond Duncan

___ **Aware of the time of day.** Audiences expect delivery and content to change with the time of day. From 7:00 a.m. to 11:00 a.m. they can easily process data, facts, figures. From around 11:00 a.m. to 2:00 p.m. they need data mixed with fluff. (Fluff in this context is stories, demonstrations, involvement, analogies, photos, props, quotes, samples, etc.) Fluff is easier to process than facts and gives the brain a break.

From mid-afternoon until 6:00, you can have an equal amount of fluff to facts. After 6:00 p.m. the ratio changes. The brain has been stressed and is weary from all the day's events. Now it needs fluff more than data.

After eating dinner and into the night, the ratio is better suited to 90:10 fluff to facts. During the evening, the brain doesn't want to have to process, deduct, and figure things out. It needs a rest. The audience now demands entertainment. An important rule for after-dinner speakers is: don't use humor unless you want to get paid for speaking.

___ **Genuine**. They want to see the same person off-stage they saw on-stage.

___ **Respectful**. In the book *Games People Play,* Dr. Eric Berne describes four possible behavior modes humans employ when relating to one another. They are:
- I'm OK — You're OK
- I'm OK — You're Not OK
- I'm Not OK — You're OK
- I'm Not OK — You're Not OK

The point is: talking to an audience is no different. They want you to feel OK and give them plenty of credit for being OK. In fact, if you sincerely think they are better than OK, you should tell them so.

___ **Sure of your close.** When you end it, you have a definite end, not a tapering off. Know your last statement as well as your first sentence. You must somehow signal to the audience that you are finished. A confident ending will sound different than if you aren't sure.

It will have a ring to it that says, "This is exactly what I wanted to say and exactly how I wanted to say it." For example: Have you ever seen musicians who were so well rehearsed, they all quit playing at exactly the same moment? Wasn't there immediate applause? Why? Because the end was signaled in such a clear and distinct manner. Contrast that experience to the time someone in the audience mistook a droning speaker's pause as a conclusion, and began applauding.

I once worked with a brilliant businessman named Greg Bustin, who owned a highly successful public relations company with many national clients. Anyone would feel proud working with such well-known customers. Greg hired me to coach 20 of his employees who were national account representatives. Together, we designed a training curriculum based on his input and on a survey of the future participants.

What impressed me the most was the direction Greg gave me the day before the training began. He said, "We do a good job one on one, serving the customer. We usually exceed their expectations. We value the relationship and the business, but when we make group presentations, we often lose our focus. I want you to emphasize one major principle throughout your instructional process, and that is this: help my people communicate how much they *love the clients* they work with." He didn't say 'like the clients they work with.' He didn't say 'suggest their affection for them.' He said *'Show them love.'* I felt like someone driving on an unfamiliar road that just spotted a road sign showing him the way to town. Greg said that the love principle, more than any other, had helped him build his enviable business.

Largely, how well you do, as a speaker will depend on how the listeners feel about themselves when you finish. – Felix Parker

I've mentioned Abraham H. Maslow, a leading proponent of the psychology of self-realization, who identified a hierarchy of human needs — food, then clothing, then shelter. Our audiences usually have those things. So give them what they really crave: acceptance and importance. Professional entertainers will often tell an audience, "I love you." Am I suggesting you float into the room full of hot air about love, peace, and goodness? No. If you don't have a hint of warm appreciation for your audience, don't tell them a lie. Just try to keep your indifference to yourself (though you will find it difficult under the scrutiny of a crowd).

How well we meet the needs of an audience determines whether or not they like us, and if they like us, they not only hear us — they pay attention to us. And if they're paying attention, they are more likely to buy our products and ideas, follow our requests and welcome our leadership.

For the three elements in speechmaking — speaker, subject, and person addressed — it is the last one, the hearer, that determines the speech's end and object. – Aristotle

Additional insights

- If people have been ordered to attend your talk, you may want to acknowledge this fact — then explore reasons why audience members could benefit personally from your session.
- Discover ahead of time what the norm is for asking and answering questions. Are listeners accustomed to asking questions during a presentation or at the end?
- Take heart in the fact that most audiences want you to succeed. Their success is linked to yours.
- Audiences are composed of people with different learning styles: some visual, some auditory, some kinetic. You have a style preference, too. Include a variety of ingredients to satisfy all three. (See Chapter 15: Variety.)

THIRTEEN

PREPARATION

Form follows function.

Preparation is a process. Just as a factory transforms raw materials into useful products, your thoughts must become ideas that are useful to your listeners. The *form* is the outline, the design of your presentation. *Function* is determined by your purpose and the type of meeting that serves it. Is it a sales presentation, planning session, panel discussion, workshop, safety meeting, toast or roast? Your purpose and the meeting format will dictate the form of your presentation. For example, "Let's get started" works well for a meeting, but poorly for a prayer or eulogy; similarly, "I am really honored to be here" won't fly if you're giving testimony as a witness.

Often the effectiveness of your presentation will depend on your delivery skills, but also on how well you can think through, then write out, then edit and organize your content. Here are the steps.

PREPARATION STEPS

Step 1: Understand audience expectations
Step 2: Combine audience expectations, your objective, and the meeting's format
Step 3: List major points, steps or concepts
Step 4: Determine the outline form
Step 5: Exemplify points and reasoning
Step 6: Add an opening and closing if necessary

Nothing is particularly hard if you divide it into small jobs.
– Ray Kroc, founder, McDonalds

Step 1: Understand audience expectations. Since you cared to learn as much as possible about your audience's expectations by seeking to understand them first (Chapter Eleven), let's look at the second step of the preparation process.

Step 2: Combine audience expectations, *your objective* and the meeting's format into your thoughts as you begin forming an outline.
Your Objective. To develop an effective outline, you must identify your purpose(s) in communicating. Which of the following most closely describes your reason for speaking?

- *To inform.* When asked to bring management up-to-date on a project, you don't want anyone to do something as a result. Your purpose is to share data and information. You are the messenger, not the salesperson; however, you do have to sell them on paying attention.
- *To persuade.* "All Smokers Should Be Banned From Restaurants!" "Pilots Deserve a 15% Pay Raise!" "Safety Is Job Number One." If you're giving talks like these, your goal is to convince your listeners not

only to hear your message, but also to accept your proposal. A persuasive speech offers a solution to a problem, by presenting sufficient logic, evidence and emotion to swing the audience to your side.

- *To instruct.* Suppose you are asked to share information on how to use the company's online training programs. You need to cover the topic so thoroughly that your listeners will come away with adequate knowledge to efficiently and comfortably navigate the system.

- *To activate (or motivate).* You want listeners to take action on your suggestion or request. You need to build an argument that will motivate them to save or acquire something.

- *To facilitate.* Leading a problem solving meeting, merging two departments, or exploring information. More on facilitation in Chapter 21.

- *To entertain.* You don't have to put on a clown suit or tell jokes to entertain. Activities are one way. Maybe conduct a tour. Show a film clip. Ask an industry celebrity to speak. Another way is to have a theme for your meeting like an advertising Super Bowl; racecars with teams as pit crews competing for recognition; horse races with pony shaped cutouts that advance on points earned in a group quiz; Olympic events with multiple winners in different categories; a treasure hunt for company principles; a survivor quiz; a cruise with a port-of-call for each module; or borrow a popular game show format.

By stating your objective clearly, you'll begin to shape the subject and tailor information to support that objective. You'll need less information and fewer visuals to make your points. Less excess information will make your points easier to remember. Your audience should leave the meeting able to articulate the thrust of your presentation and the key concepts that support it.

Even after an objective has been determined, central themes or messages are sometimes barely visible. How do you uncover them? These two exercises can help:

    i.   Pretend you just boarded an elevator heading up. Before the doors open on the 10th floor, you must state your goal and three main supporting ideas — out loud! GO!

   ii.   Grab a business card. Turn it over. In your normal handwriting, write and edit the goal until it is concise enough to fit on the back of the card. On a second card, write the three main supporting ideas.

Chance favors the prepared mind. – Louis Pasteur

Meeting Formats (see facing page). These are listed because formats have expected protocols and designs. When you choose a format, you acknowledge its characteristics in your overall approach. It also helps your listeners understand the purpose better and reduces excuses like "If I had known what kind of meeting we were having, I would have prepared better," or "I don't understand why we're really getting together." When possible, state a specific meeting format. People will pay more attention to your agenda if the reason for getting together is more than just "another meeting."

To experience freedom, seek structure.

Step 3: List major points, steps or concepts.

Brainstorm a list of key points, examples and concepts. Get everything important about your subject on paper. Here order doesn't matter, *quantity* does: you can organize, add, and omit later. Take a fresh sheet of paper. Leave space at the top and bottom, and triple space between concepts as you jot them down. Describe each point in as few words as possible. Write concise 'mind-joggers,' not sentences.

Fearless and Persuasive Speaking

1. Formal keynote speech
2. Board meeting presentation
3. Stockholders meeting
4. Teambuilding session
5. Training workshop
6. Green-light creative brainstorming session
7. Question and answer session
8. Problem-solving session
9. Panel of experts
10. Team presentation
11. Project meeting
12. Sales report
13. Safety meeting
14. Cross-training
15. Systems procedure
16. Kickoff meeting
17. Mentor-mentee meeting
18. Orientation
19. Members forum
20. Introducing a new product or service
21. Merger or acquisition planning
22. Goal setting
23. Goal celebration
24. Organizational meeting
25. Department meeting
26. Breakfast meeting
27. Luncheon
28. After-dinner speech
29. Testimonial
30. Sales meeting
31. Sales support meeting
32. Budget meeting
33. Banquet
34. Self-introduction
35. Book review
36. Recognition ceremony
37. Holiday party
38. Roast
39. Yearly, quarterly meeting
40. Progress report

Ken Bradford

Words written to be read are different
from words written to be spoken.

Step 4: Determine the outline form.

This is the *body* of the work, not the clever attention-getting opener, nor the close. The specific outline to be used will still depend on your unique purpose, the audience's expectations, the meeting format and the desired length. At this point, you might want to narrow your focus. If you need to cover more than you think the audience can bear in the time allotted, plan for an additional meeting.

For example, if your five-minute speech really needs to be a half-day training session, then use the five minutes to point out the necessity of a training session at a better time. On the other hand, if you have a mountain of information but only 10 minutes to cover it, stick to the format, but cover the major points instead of each detail. Consider providing a handout with complete details.

Below are some proven outline suggestions:
1. *Past, Present, Future.* It worked pretty well for Lincoln at Gettysburg. "Fourscore and seven years ago" (the past, paraphrased); "now we are engaged..." (the present); "The world will little note..." (the future).
2. *Three Major Points.* Most governments, religions and wonders of the world are established around a three-point configuration. Listeners can easily absorb three points. Four seems cumbersome unless they are united in a memorable way, like with an acronym.
3. *When, Where, Who, What, How, Why?* An experienced reporter knows to ask these questions when covering a story. If you ask the same questions of yourself, you will do a nice job of informing the audience.

4. *Situation, Possible Causes, Possible Solutions, Best Possible Solution, Plan of Action.* This is the scientific formula approach to problem solving.

5. *Pros, Cons, Conclusion.* Weighing both sides of an issue and deciding an answer.

6. *The Conclusion.* Begin with the end result and list each main point that advances thought in the reaching of it.

7. *A List of Priorities.* Start with the highest priority. Emphasis is not on completing the list, but on accomplishing chief concerns first.

8. *Technical Configuration.* For instance, the relationship of hardware, software and printer.

9. *Spatial Context.* Dividing the outline into parts. For example, when you are describing the inside and outside of a motor; or exterior and interior of a building.

10. *Flow.* How a system or process functions by following the flow of energy being transmitted and transformed.

Make an ugly outline. In the basement of the Ford's Theatre in Washington, D.C., the original outline of the Gettysburg Address is on display, all seven messy and heavily edited copies of the proclamation. Your outline will likely need the same work as Lincoln's — a little time and editing.

I would have written you a shorter letter, but I didn't have time.
– Mark Twain

Remember, your subject should be addressed as a logical order of ideas that stay on target with your purpose, form and function. There is no one correct outline or agenda, but you and your audience will follow the path you lay out, so keep it clear and straightforward. You'll use this outline to rehearse your presentation.

Ken Bradford

Step 5: Exemplify points and reasoning

1. Know how to make your points memorable, interesting and believable.
2. Find the hard numbers that serve as evidence rather than opinions. Perhaps quote the source.
3. Do extra homework. Go get a new firsthand experience with the subject.
4. How about using a prop or showing an actual sample?
5. Would an illustration (drawing, photo, sketch, diagram) work better than a statement?
6. Use a variety of ways to make your points and break up monotonous facts.

Step 6: Add an opening and closing if necessary.

If an opener is needed, it needs to accomplish three things.

1. Capture favorable attention
2. Be relevant to the subject
3. Be brief

Closing segments can also play an important role in delivery; however, it's a mistake to believe that you always need to review all the points you've made. Again, the function will usually dictate whether or not to summarize, call to action, vote, take a break, compliment the group, thank them, or blow kisses. And since you may be presenting as a team you will not always be the last to speak, thus negating a closing comment. Common sense says to know how you want to close before you get there, so it's best to plan it.

The fact you are reading this chapter indicates that you want the best for yourself and your audience. As with most endeavors — how much we prepare shows how much we care.

Fearless and Persuasive Speaking

More important than the will to win, is the willingness to prepare to win. – Bobby Knight

Additional insights

Content is important, but you also need to prepare yourself and everything you can control about the room where you will be speaking. Recently, a friend of mine spent over three hours preparing the content of her address for her annual association convention. Her notes contained the names of 20 people she wanted to acknowledge for having made sizable contributions to the association.

Once behind the lectern, she panicked. Not because she hadn't prepared her speech, but because she didn't know that a little switch could be turned on the lectern lamp to see her notes. She shared with me later how the fear had caused her to mumble something and hastily sit down after only a few seconds.

The point: Go early. Test equipment. Change whatever you can about the room that needs improving, like closing the blinds on an active window, rearranging chairs, or moving the lectern.

Accept what you can't change. Then do what most audiences would do with the unexpected: ask for help, laugh, or go on!

FOURTEEN
REHEARSING

It's never the first time for the real audience.

Most of us have put on a school play. When I was in the second grade, our class was studying nutrition, so we became posters with fruit and vegetables drawn on them. I was a carrot, and I was proud to be a member of a major food group.

For two days straight we practiced in the auditorium instead of going outside for recess. The play was pretty simple, even for second graders. All the kids were to circle around the stage twice and then stand together with other kids in their food group. Each young thespian declared what vitamins and minerals were found in their item. Even without much rehearsal, the audience probably could have figured out the concept; but because we rehearsed, we presented the two dozen different fruits, vegetables, milk products and grains in an orderly fashion and clearly communicated the specific benefits to the listeners.

I can still feel the excitement as the purple auditorium curtain was hauled open and we looked into the sea of faces. I imagine it was a big deal to the teacher, too. This second-grade play was probably *the* event of the year for our class, but it was especially important that day–because our parents were coming!

Last year, I recalled my second-grade play as I listened to an advertising C.E.O. complain about the performance of his account managers. They had recently done an annual review for one of their biggest clients, a national baking company. The purpose of the presentation had been to review the past year's marketing campaign. Their presentation hadn't gone well; at best, it had finished in second place. Since there was only room in the budget for first-place finishers, the advertising firm had lost the account, along with $10,000,000 to a competitor's presentation team.

The losing presenters knew that there had been little cohesiveness to the hour-long presentation. It had lacked a central message, substantiating points, enough specific facts, clear benefits and enthusiasm. Experience wasn't the problem faced by the presenters. The three reps had over 20 years of experience giving presentations. So why the dismal results? As you have probably guessed, the trio had never rehearsed.

If our parents had been worth two rehearsals back in the second grade, isn't your audience worth a couple of rehearsals now?

Rehearsal means something different for everyone. For some it's a quick glance at a few key ideas on paper and then on to the meeting. For others it's an all-day and sometimes into the night "memory-a-thon." Obviously, the goal is to rehearse as little as possible in order to become organized and competent. Practice may not make the presentation perfect, but it always improves it.

Rehearsing to win

Just as great athletes visualize themselves breaking barriers, great communicators rehearse in order to visualize their successes. Why, then, do a remarkable number of presenters seem to do their best to avoid rehearsals before giving a major presentation? I have heard many different reasons: for example, that rehearsal stifles creativity and creates "robot" presenters. Others beg for more time to prepare, until there isn't any time left to practice. Still others worry so much about giving a "perfect" presentation every time that they will not practice for fear of making a mistake.

Rehearsal roadblocks can be overcome. Here are some suggestions.

1. **Feeling like you are "not quite ready"** to rehearse is the reason to rehearse. If we wait until we "feel" ready, without practicing, the time may never come. Action is the quickest and surest way to feel at ease with our words.

2. **Schedule at least three rehearsals** prior to a major pitch. The first rehearsal is a walk-through where the participants talk about what they are going to say and become familiar with the continuity and progression of their remarks. The second practice session should be without visual aids; the last, a full dress rehearsal.

3. **Your goal is to "be present"** with the audience. If you believe that rehearsing could stifle your spontaneity, you may be creating a self-fulfilling prophecy. Without rehearsing, you might be more dependent on notes that increase the mechanicalness of your delivery.

4. **If you feel that presenting means memorizing** words and movements so you can deliver a speech verbatim, then you will limit yourself to being an uninteresting, uninspiring speaker. True creativity in presentations comes from a presenter who is alert, who reacts with the audience, and who encourages impromptu situations where something he or she says has created a contact or interaction with the audience.

5. **If you pay too much attention to saying each and every word just right** — you may not be able pay much attention to the audience and their reactions.

The amount of practice necessary is dictated by the form and function of the event. Let's look at eight common speaking scenarios as we discuss rehearsing.

-   Brief prepared comments for a meeting
-   Impromptu talk
-   Formal speech
-   Sales presentation
-   Panel discussion
-   Workshop or training session
-   Introduction
-   TV, radio or teleconference interview

Brief prepared comments for a meeting

A frequent speaking situation is the weekly meeting at the office. It's usually a mixture of informality and serious business that needs to be covered.

1. First, get your thoughts on paper. Don't worry about order. Avoid writing out full sentences because you're not going to read them aloud anyway. You want brief notes so you can focus on delivery and be yourself.
2. Next, prioritize your key points. One of the quickest and easiest ways to arrange your thoughts is by using the three-point outline. (See Ch. 13: Preparation.) It's an excellent choice for quick preparation and rehearsal.
3. Before the meeting begins, go over the handful of pertinent points until two things happen:
    a. You can easily give the talk each time you practice, almost without looking at your notes, and

b. You can picture the main points in your mind and know their sequence. An acronym is a great crutch to help you remember key ideas. For example, I use the letters "A-C-E" to help me explain three speaking elements: Awareness, Content, and Energy. Prepare your key points vertically on a note card or sheet of paper like this:

A – Awareness
C – Content
E – Energy

4. Large bold vertical print is easier to read than crowded words in sentence form. (Scientists have found that speech notes actually shrink two full font sizes when the speaker is using them.)
5. Don't crowd words onto a page to try to save paper. Your goal is to have white space frame the words in print.
6. Don't memorize sentences. You want to sound competent, not stilted. If you memorize, you risk someone derailing your train of thought with a question or interruption.
7. Speak from key points and from your own experience.

Impromptu talk

Unplanned speeches, made up on the spur of the moment, can be dangerous. In the tense moments as you prepare to stand and say something intelligent — consider the following ideas:

1. Rather than generalizing and rambling, recall a specific incident from your own experience. Describe the memory. It's much easier than making up lofty sentences.
2. Appeal to noble motives. Talking about values you share with the audience is a safe route. For example, unselfish service is a fundamental principle for most civic groups.

3. On your way to the meeting, anticipate topics that could be discussed.
4. If in doubt, speak from the heart.

It usually takes me a good two weeks to prepare an impromptu speech. – Mark Twain

Formal speech

Rehearse with your notes the same way you practiced giving short comments. List the key concepts in a vertical column down the left-hand side of an 8 ½ x 11 page, triple spacing between thoughts.

It's a good idea to take your notes with you to the presentation even if you don't plan to use them. If you want to call less attention to them, put your notes on the lectern prior to the start of the meeting. Once there, you can use them only if needed, like a life raft aboard a ship. An alternative is to stand to the side of the lectern with your notes on the edge of the stand. This way you can get out from behind the lectern and still glance at your notes as needed.

Once you have your outline prepared, decide how you will emphasize each point. (See Chapter 15: Variety.) For example, for your first point you could start with a brief, attention-getting story. Don't write the entire story on a sheet of paper; just boil it down to one or two words or "memory joggers" that can bring it to the front of your mind. If this doesn't work for you, then practice telling the story a few times to willing friends or small animals. Time spent commuting by car can be used for practice, except when you're at stoplights.

For your second point, you might use an analogy or slide to illustrate the concept. Remember, variety helps hold attention and provides a different angle of understanding.

Legal notices, expert witness statements, and press announcements are among items that should be read to assure accuracy. The only other times you should read verbatim is when using a direct quote, reciting several numbers or giving technical details.

Poems add diversity to your speech, but keep them short. If you have a longer poem you want to use, shorten it by setting the scene in your own words then read the pertinent stanzas. The point is: read as little as possible.

Notes should help you express yourself, not bog you down or hide your personality. Here are some suggestions:

- **Use 4 x 6 (rather than 3 x 5)** cards or 8 ½ x 11 notepaper. The fewer pieces of paper you have, the better, especially if they get out of order or they're dropped. Write on only one side of each sheet and number your pages. As you finish a page, slide it to the side. Forget the staple.
- **Key words** should be surrounded by lots of white space, not tons of text. After you refer to your notes, look up. Speak to the group. Never talk to an inanimate object — for very long!
- **Bold** the words that you wish to emphasize. Add marks like these /// to remind you to pause.
  / =one second pause, // = two seconds, etc.
- **Use all caps sparingly.** They're usually overkill. AFTER ALL, NOTHING STANDS OUT IF EVERYTHING IS CAPITALIZED.
- **Use "key concepts"** as guides. These concepts should prompt you to speak from your own experience and use your own examples. If you have no experience, do what a reporter would do: Go get the story and make some notes.
- **Practice** as if you're trying to convince your mother, and be on the lookout for too many tongue twisters and yawn-makers. Over use of words that end in "-tion" and "-ize" dulls the ear. (Their utilization also cannibalizes your enunciation!) Edit sentences to "earable," understandable words. Use your spell-check software to communicate at a junior-high rather than dissertation level.

Ken Bradford

Sales presentation

Your *sales* presentation should be written in a persuasive form that follows the psychological steps of the *buying* process. There are many varieties, but all have the following points in common:
- First, get an audience's favorable attention.
- Second, talk about what they are interested in.
- Third, share convincing evidence instead of mere opinions.
- Fourth, nurture a desire to buy by describing audience members in future situations where they are already using or benefiting from your suggestions.
- Fifth, ask for action. Close.

If you plan to use slides, remember: you want more than a slide show. You want people to remember you and your face. If you're standing over to the side of the room in the dark, your audience will not connect with you and no trust will be built. Practice staying connected visually and emotionally with the audience. Face the audience, not the slide screen. Stand and never sit when presenting to a group. You are there to lead, not to be a slide technician.

Finally, never forget: *"You are the message."*– Roger Ailes

Additional sales presentation tips

- **Be flexible.** Sometimes the presentation is not an all-or-nothing event, but rather part of a larger process of discovery. Be open to taking questions at any point, or know how to postpone them tactfully.
- **Buying is both a logical an emotional process.** People may say they make decisions out of logic, but ingredients like pride, fear, and comfort and are usually part of the mix. Consider how each segment of your presentation addresses the psychological and emotional needs of the audience.

- **Try to predict** audience objections and consider the value of answering some of them before they arise.
- **Practice** your answers beforehand.

Perfect speakers exist only in educational films.
—Terry L. Paulson

Panel discussions

- When presenting as a member of a team, practice your part, but organize it around the larger purpose.
- Don't try to cover everything you know. Focus on areas most pertinent to the topic.
- You may be expected to speak anywhere from three to ten minutes on your area of expertise. Ask the moderator for guidelines.
- Listen as the other panelists speak. Focus on them to avoid distracting the audience. Remember, you are sharing the stage.
- Create one or two serious questions to ask the audience. Audiences often enjoy being brought into the discussion.
- Read the newspaper the day of the program to stay in touch with the most current events.

Workshop or training session

- As in the above situations, the key is to become familiar with what comes next in your remarks, but in terms of modules rather than key concepts.
- Consider making the handout and your sequence notes the same. Just add your crib notes to your copy. Establish time marks. Estimate the length of each module and strive to stay on target. As you gain experience conducting the session, adjust the time periods to meet your needs. Allow time for plenty of interaction.

- Create transitions to help conclude segments and to bring participants' attention back after a break. (See Chapter 21: Facilitating)

Making introductions

Here is a simple formula.
1. **Announce the topic** so everyone knows they're in the right room at the right time.
2. **Give the name** of the presenter and title of the remarks.
3. **Tell the audience** why they will want to hear this person on this topic. Your job is to set the stage, to stir them from neutral to anticipation.
4. **Give examples** of how this person has earned respect in his/her field (rather than a laundry list of credentials) or relate a very brief story to show his/her expertise. People usually relate better to people than to degrees or dates of tenure.
5. **Bring on the speaker** by saying his/her name again and using a sweeping gesture motioning him or her to come to the podium. Do not leave the podium until the speaker has arrived. An empty stage can cause the audience's attention span to wander.
6. **Lead the applause.**
7. **Keep the introduction short.** More than 90 seconds is usually too long. Shoot for less than one minute.

Television, radio, or teleconference interview

- Rehearse by fully writing out questions you would like to answer. Give these to the host a day before the program is to take place. They may or may not use them.
- Anticipate additional questions the host may ask you. Practice your answers.
- Days before your interview listen to the program and famil-

iarize yourself with the format and the host's style.
- Go early to the station to avoid feeling rushed and to get comfortable with the set and equipment.

Post-rehearsal launch sequence

FIVE: You're dressed in clothes that make you feel good and are right for the occasion.

FOUR: You've arrived early enough to check the room setup, the equipment, and greet some folks. Take a calm moment to rehearse your opening sentence and key points.

THREE: Monitor your inner voice. Replace any talk like "I hope I don't forget something," or "I hope they like me," with "I know what I'm talking about. They wouldn't have asked me to speak if they didn't want to hear what I have to say. I'm ready! I'm okay. They're okay. We're all equals." Take yourself lightly. Give yourself permission to enjoy the experience.

TWO: Check posture. Breathe deeply and fully without straining.

ONE: Smile as you listen to the nice introduction you wrote.

ENGAGE: Rise and walk to the front like the winner you are!

Remember: A single presentation isn't going to make or break a career, but a good performance makes you someone to watch.

Before everything else, getting ready is the secret of success. – Henry Ford

Additional insights

- Videotaping your performance can accelerate your progress. As difficult as it is to watch yourself, what you learn makes the next performance easier and more effective.
- Get grounded. Practice what you preach, so you can preach what you practice.

- Despite centuries of well-meaning advice, avoid mirrors except to check your image.
- Never read your opening sentence, especially if it's saying your name. The audience's first impression will be, "This speaker wouldn't miss us if we all left now."
- Be willing to sacrifice perfection for warmth. Most of the time, it's okay to say things a bit differently each time you speak.
- It's fine to have notes in your hand while speaking, but if your hands are shaking, leave your notes on the lectern.

FIFTEEN

VARIETY

If the audience doesn't change every few minutes, the show should.

If it were a punishable offense to conduct dull meetings, a large portion of corporate America would be permanently behind bars.

By far the most frequently and flagrantly violated principle in this book is that of variety. When anything looks, sounds, or moves in a repetitive fashion, it kills interest. Sameness is fatal, yet way too many meetings these days sound, look, and smell the same … boring, boring, boring.

Ironically, though most people hate to attend uninspiring meetings, when it's their turn to stand up, they play it safe and deliver their message no differently than their peers. At Monday's meeting Joe is wishing for a fire alarm to put an end to a presenter's sleep-inducing slides. At Tuesday's he's up front, trying desperately to make an impact with his own deadly set.

Ken Bradford

I wondered why somebody didn't do something: then I realized that I was somebody. – Anonymous

Just because other professionals always make their presentations using fifteen to twenty slides with four to six bullet points each doesn't mean yours should do the same. Listeners like organized information, but they also like variety.

A physiologist who took my course said that the human mind likes change, but it *loves chaos and order* at the same time. Think about it — football games have specific rules and boundaries, but at any given moment with 22 people running at full steam, anything can happen. Other examples of chaos and order working together are amusement park rides, action-adventure movies, and television game shows. What does that mean to you as a speaker? Simply this: if the audience remains the same, the show needs to change every few minutes (hinting at chaos) to hold the viewers' attention. Obviously, if the audience changes, like Broadway theater patrons, the show can remain the same each night, but it still needs to have a variety of scenes.

The folks at Ringling Brothers, Barnum and Bailey Circus have long understood how to mix chaos and order effectively. Why three rings, when it's impossible to focus on more than one at a time? Because, from the start, the Ringling brothers knew how variety could hold an audience's attention. Some acts were on the ground, some in the air. Some were funny, some scary. Some were viewed in fast motion, others in slow motion ... you get the idea. And the only overhead in sight is the high-wire act.

Am I suggesting that you wear red tights and fire yourself from a cannon during the next shareholder meeting? Although it would certainly liven things up, that's not the kind of visibility you're looking for. But do ask yourself, as you prepare your next talk, if developing yet another slide-dominated program is really the most powerful method you can use to make an impact. The answer might be yes. But then again, it might be no.

Even if you've included some spectacular multi-media visual aids, what about your spoken text? How many times have you, as an audience member, felt the deflating shift as the program turned from a dazzling electronic presentation to a tiresome talking head?

> *"The goal is to finish before they do."*
> – Professor Warren Quinlan

An engineer once told me, "I finally have my presentation down."

"How so?" I asked.

"Because my friend is going to help me with the slides. It's a 30-minute presentation, so he'll change it for me every 17 seconds," he replied.

"How many slides do you intend to use?" I inquired.

"108."

He had managed to organize monotony to the nth degree. Of course, each slide contained a different idea, but the delivery process was better suited to an assembly line. I didn't bother asking him what would happen if someone from the audience 'interrupted' with a question.

Even entire cities can experience problems if they ignore the value of variety. For example, in the 1950s, traffic lights in Galveston, Texas, were synchronized to allow drivers who maintained a constant speed of 40 miles an hour an uninterrupted green light commute during rush hour. Traffic moved better, but not without a high cost. The number of accidents in the area soon doubled. People were literally driving off the road for no apparent reason. Consultants were called in to figure out what was going on.

It seems that on either side of the main highway there were rows and rows of beautiful palm trees. Every 30 feet for seven miles. At sunrise and near sunset, the prime commute time and new peak accident time, these trees resembled strobe lights, casting an alternate, repetitive pattern of shadow and sunlight into the eyes of drivers. To solve the problem, the city cut down enough trees to create a random pattern. Soon drivers were on their way again, without taking annoying detours into sandbars as they drove to and from work.

Keep the moral of this story in mind as you prepare your next speech. Avoid predictable, mechanical repetitions of any kind. I hear many more speeches than the average person, but I've always got plenty of company in la-la land when I hear the predictable click of the keyboard between slides, the lights are down low, and the speaker's voice is a soft and monotone.

There is no one best way to keep attention or add variety, but the following ideas, given potency by your own creativity, personality, and circumstances, should help.

Change sites. New surroundings help to keep the audience's priorities in focus. Campbell Soup's chairman Gordon McGovern once held a board meeting in the back room of a supermarket. After the meeting, the board members roamed the aisles to get shoppers' comments about their products.

Let the audience move. One way is to have them respond to a question with a show of hands or, more dramatically, have them all stand, then ask a question that they answer by sitting down. For example: "If you have ever made up an excuse to get out of a speaking engagement — sit down." You could follow with "Those who are still standing will now choose one person from those seated to come up here and speak on a topic of your choice. No, just kidding, but I personally know what it is like to try to keep from doing something I wasn't comfortable with, and I can see by your response that I must not be alone."

Let the audience refresh. Call a break. Clap your hands to regain attention after a noisy break. For example, "If you can hear the sound of my voice, clap once." Clap once. "If you can hear the sound of my voice, clap twice!" Clap twice. " If you can hear the sound of my voice, clap three times!" Clap three times. By this point, you will usually have everyone in the room quiet.

You move, but do so with purpose. See Chapter 5: Movement.

Create props. Relevant props are a welcome relief to observers. I use a boomerang to help explain how our "criticism of others" returns to harm us. At the hardware store, I bought a three-foot length of electrical cord with plugs on each end to use when talking about a speaker "connecting" with an audience. Don't just rely on those old standbys: slides and overhead projectors. (See Chapter 11: Visuals) Always be on the search for a new prop that could add impact to a favorite idea.

Shift to a true personal story. Use your experiences to create an example. You can gain the audience's involvement by telling a good descriptive story with a relevant point that involves listeners mentally as well emotionally. If you have a good one in mind, but it's 10 minutes long, use it anyway after you have edited it down to one minute. Remember that a point is often better made with fewer words than too many. (See Chapter 18: Stories)

Stories are the spices that change a bland address into a tasty presentation. – Hal Copeland

Use an anecdote. An anecdote doesn't have to be a personal story, just one that makes a point. For example, a story like *The Emperor's New Clothes,* you hear a simple story, but you get a deeper principle. Anecdotes were said to be Lincoln's favorite speaking tool. He had hundreds written down. From time to time, we all hear good anecdotes. The key is to record them somehow, so you can use one when the time is right.

Announce a "pop" quiz. To create understanding, not panic; announce a pop test. The answers could come from the material you just covered or from the subject you are about to talk about.

Make a spontaneous sketch on the flipchart or dry-erase board. Bring your words to life with a simple drawing or notation. Don't omit this wonderful tool, because you can't draw like Michelangelo. Just remember to keep it extremely simple and large. The acronym to keep in mind is K.I.L.L. Keep it large and legible.

Use an analogy. An analogy makes a useful comparison of something that the audience is already familiar with, to something you are introducing. (See Chapter: 19 Persuasion)

Create a demonstration. There's a good reason for so many cooking shows on television. People love demonstrations. If you can show what you mean, it is far more effective than just talking about it. For added punch, use an audience member as part of the show.

Design a role-play module. Role-playing creates variety, involvement, empathy and greater understanding. Beyond the initial "moans" sometimes offered by volunteers, it is a welcome twist to many programs.

Insert a quote. Quotes grab attention and are more interesting than plain text. They also demonstrate the fact that you did your homework.

Record audience input on a flipchart. Then honor them even more by posting the sheets on the wall and leaving them up. Remember how Mom honored our work by posting it on the door of the refrigerator? Capturing the group synergy is usually a great idea. All will take pride in having contributed and your program will benefit from the richness of many different perspectives.

Ask the group for an example rather than giving one of your own. Recently, I related two of my favorite examples to the audience, and then I asked for one of theirs. Result? I heard six additional examples on my topic.

Occasionally dumb up. Instead of answering a question the way you always do, pause and put the question to the audience, saying, "I would like to hear what you think about that…" Radio talk show hosts use this technique to make their phone lines ring.

Change the pace. All programs have a tempo. Be aware of yours, especially if you are doing a longer program. One way to change the pace is to ask something like, "Would everyone take out a sheet of paper and write down one useful idea that they have gotten so far." Then add, "Let's take 30 seconds to jot it on paper, and then we'll listen to as many as possible, before we take a break." Change gears again by gathering the thoughts with a sense of urgency.

Use music to start your program or bring people back into the room after a break.

Make a poster. Remember how Former President Reagan used a poster during a State-of-the-Union address (Chapter Eleven) to explain how inflation was affected by supply and demand. He could have used an overhead, but he wanted a simple, hand-held chart. It was the first time any president had even chosen to display a poster on television. The next day the press christened him "The Great Communicator."

Costumes, decorations, and musical instruments? Maybe so! One of the most memorable sales meetings I ever attended was when the president of the company and two sales managers danced into the meeting wearing trench coats, dark sunglasses, and playing toy saxophones – to the recorded sound of *I'm A Soul*

Man. They substituted the word "Sold" for "Soul". Frankly, we all were laughing so hard that we couldn't hear the full script. They were smart to insert this bit during the lull of the afternoon. What an energy boost for everyone!

One of my students told me about a meeting she attended in Mexico City. Her role was to introduce the president of the company who had come down from America to visit the Mexican division of the company. Over 400 local employees attended. Just as she finished delivering a short introduction, the back door of the meeting room burst open, and in came 30 Mariachi singers with guitars. They played a welcome song for the visiting official. She said the president was overwhelmed by the hospitality produced by the ensemble. It also helped demonstrate how the Mexican employees valued the relationship with their U.S. partners. For me, it emphasized how variety is limited only to the imagination.

It's not hard to understand why variety is important. Statistics show that the average person's attention span is growing shorter, not longer. We live in the era of the six-second sound bite. Anything longer in the news script and we don't listen well. We want our information quickly. When frequent movement and change is lacking, we click the channel changer. It's nothing for us to change 160 channels, throw the channel changer aside and say, "There's nothing on."

It's a challenge to gain and hold an audience's attention, but these techniques should help prevent your words from becoming monotonous. Your listeners will stay tuned-in to your message because the changes in your delivery will keep them wondering what's coming next. Variety with purpose is the key.

Variety is still the spice of life.
– McCormick

Additional insights

- The purpose of variety is not merely entertainment. It's to gain and hold attention so you can better explain and persuade.
- The least expensive variety is the spectrum of your personality, when you allow it to show through enthusiasm.
- The ability to create laughter and then touch the listeners' hearts is a wonderful mix. (See Chapter 17: Humor & Chapter 3: Vulnerability)
- As you prepare, instead of always asking yourself, "What am I going to say?" try " What am I going to have them do?"
- We all need a change of air sometimes, like the dog that pokes his head out of a moving car. Variety makes us grateful, and audiences show gratitude by accepting your message and acting on it.

SIXTEEN

EXAMPLES

If you're missing examples — your audience may be missing the point.

Don't make the all-too-common mistake of forgetting that your audience, no matter how important, is still made up of human beings who identify with people, not with abstractions like "profitability" or "implementation."

Recently, I was coaching a client on what had gone wrong with a presentation he made to the engineering department at his firm. His subject was the importance of education. Here is how it began:

> *We've set sail for a new world — one that opens up tremendous opportunities. But the weather is unpredictable, the maps are inadequate and even the compass*

is a bit suspect. If we are successful in our knowledge-management efforts, the constraints of the past will wither and the potential for accomplishment and achievement will greatly expand. Such advances, of course, will demand a commitment to learning — and unlearning.

Here is how the talk could have been written, using examples:

Last year, our company completed $475,000,000 worth of new construction in the Northwest corridor of Franklin County. It is estimated that next year over 150 new businesses will be relocating to this area. We want to increase our business by 25%, but to do this we need to work smart as well as hard. That's why I am suggesting we raise our minimum continuing education requirements from 40 hours a year to 50.

My client's speech continued:

Knowledge has become the "key resource" of the world economy. The chief assets of an organization are no longer its physical or financial assets, but, rather, its intellectual assets. While speed, agility, and collaboration with colleagues and customers will certainly help determine which companies succeed in the marketplace, leading-edge mindwork will lie at the heart of nearly all future success stories.

A suggested translation using examples:

Last year we won the $86 million Orlando airport radar systems job by being the only project team among five other bidding companies that could answer questions about the construction of Doppler radar systems. Our presentation team had just completed a National Air

Safety Radar Construction class. Education gave us the winning edge.

To make matters worse, when it came time for him to speak, the facilitator informed him that he had only five minutes instead of ten, so he hurriedly read his speech, leaving off the last two pages. Had he been speaking from examples instead of from text, he could have whittled them down to make his main points.

Notice the difference in the two examples. Gone from each of the latter are the long and flabby nouns of generalized meaning. In their place are the short words and vivid images from everyday life — the crunch of real numbers, the race, and the battle.

Plain talk is not easily achieved in corporate America, where so much vanity is on the line. Executives and mangers at every level are prisoners of the myth that a simple style reflects a simple mind.

Remember, a simple style is actually the result of hard work and hard thinking. A muddled style is the reflection of a person who is unable or too lazy to organize his thoughts.

It is simplicity that makes the uneducated more effective than the educated when addressing popular audiences.
-Aristotle

Opinion vs. fact

Knowing the difference between an opinion and a fact can give your words an edge. An opinion is subjective, reflecting your opinion only, while a fact is provable and less arguable. Examples that illustrate your intellectual points add the credibility of fact to whatever you are trying to show or prove. Examples will:

- **Show** your depth of understanding
- **Prove** relevancy

- **Clarify** your meaning
- **Save** time persuading
- **Show** preparedness
- **Display** your leadership skills.

Examples paint mind pictures.

People want to see what you are talking about in their minds. Audiences loathe a presentation filled with generalities. Descriptive examples stimulate listener's minds, because they create moving images,rather like a play or movie. Our minds love changing images.

What is an incident?

As opposed to a generality, an incident is a specific occurrence, recalling a particular point in history. It might invoke a specific event in the storyteller's life. For example: your first date. Unless you've had only one date, dating is a generality. How you spent your 21st or 40th birthday was an incident. Can't think of a single example? Then create one by getting out of your office and proving your point first-hand.

One thorn of experience is worth a whole wilderness of warning.
– James Russell Lowell

Details focus the image.

Just as the adjustment knobs on your television control the brightness, contrast and sharpness on the screen, you can control the image you paint for listeners by the verbal distinctions you make. With a little effort, vague pronouns can become proper names. "Them" can be changed to "my dad's twin brothers Herald and Jerald;" "us" can become "our fifth grade football team — the War Eagles, from Waurika, Oklahoma." The key is in answering questions that a reporter would ask. Give your audience the WHEN, WHERE, WHO, WHAT, WHY, & HOW? of your first project or your most memorable accomplishment. Television reporters would be out of news and out of business without these six questions to frame their stories:

- **When?** Rather than say, "the other day" try "the middle of last week."
- **Where?** Instead of "a small town" use its real name. Maybe it was "Cotton Center" or "Round Rock." Proper names bring pictures to mind.
- **Who?** Be specific. Instead of "some people" try "an elderly man from Jamaica, named Poppy, and his six year old granddaughter."
- **What?** Rather than say, "something happened" say "at about 7:50 a.m. I walked up the sidewalk in front of my building and saw a crowd of my friends and co-workers reading from a large poster which said Closed Due to Bankruptcy."
- **Why?** Tell us the motive or reason for the action in your story.
- **How?** Describe how you felt during the incident, i.e., "heartbroken," "frustrated," "overwhelmed," "despairing," "jubilant."

Your first resource for examples

Start with your own background. Reflect on specific, personal incidents that exemplify the point you want to make. Here are some tools to help you search your worldly experience, so you can come up with good eyewitness examples. Ask yourself:

1. What's a lesson life has taught me about this subject?
2. What particular incident surrounding this idea will I always remember?

3. When was a time I was impressed by someone living this principle?
4. What was a similar challenge I faced one time, and how did I overcome such a huge obstacle?
5. How did this subject first come up?
6. What experts have I met on this subject?
7. Where have I experienced a poor example of this idea?

I have learned silence from the talkative, toleration from the intolerant, and kindness from the unkind.
— Kahlil Gibran

The interest factor

When you are talking about something *interesting to you,* you increase the possibility that it will become *interesting to the audience.* One way to tell if an incident is interesting to you is to look at how long you've kept it in your memory. If it is unforgettable, it probably still interests you. On the flip side, if you are not interested in your topic, it's pretty hard to get your audience interested. In fact, don't try. Let someone else speak.

Notice how the best speakers you know interweave stories of human struggle and decision-making to add insight and understanding to their points. But don't neglect your first resource — your own experience. Few people recognize how many incidents they have stored that can add credibility to their opinions. To find your best examples, look at the values you cherish now and search your memory for examples that illustrate their meaning to you.

An example is the best way to make any idea clearer, more interesting and persuasive. I suggest using more than just one to support your major points. The audience often appreciates your point in proportion to the different ways they experience it.

Fearless and Persuasive Speaking

Few things are harder to put up with than the annoyance of a good example. –Mark Twain

Additional insights

- Not only does the example teach, it also sells.
- All else being equal, the person speaking from a relevant example is usually more powerful than the person with nothing more than an opinion.
- Imagine every audience is asking you the six reporter's questions of When, Where, What, Who, Why, and How.
- Quoting someone else's words adds details and increases interest.
- It's okay to tell stories about yourself unless you sound like you're bragging or trying to appear superior to the listeners.
- Do extra homework. Know more about your subject than the audience. Add to their knowledge with relevant examples. *If you would lift me up — you must first be on higher ground.*

SEVENTEEN

HUMOR

You *can* learn humor, probably.

Every artist was first an amateur.
– RalphWaldo Emerson

Humor is the secret weapon of the speaker. It's secret because few presenters realize that it is often their best tool — and sometimes their only tool — for making an important point.

Can you learn to be funny? Probably, but you can certainly learn to develop the sense of humor you were born with. Most everyone can laugh when something humorous happens, but tickling others' funny bones on cue, whenever you want to, is serious business, because humor is both elusive and subjective.

Dying's tough, but it's not as tough as comedy.
– A.E. Matthews, on his deathbed.

Certainly business is one area where the right humor can produce more sales, lift morale, and lighten the workload. Laughing is an emotional experience, releasing mental and physical pressure, a welcome relief to most people. Of course, some folks find no use for humor — ever. They are obviously God's gift to mankind — as targets for levity.

The surest mark of an inner adequacy is
the operation of a sense of humor. – T.U. Smith

What's so funny?

Humor is what happens when a train of thought takes a new direction: one that's absurd or pleasantly surprising.

Comedy is the craft of examining situations and molding them into a humorous perspective expressed in condensed sentences. To see things from this humorous viewpoint, you must release the left-side of your brain, the logical side, and permit the right-side to playfully create.

In public speaking, humor is used to imbed the message. Used successfully, humor greases the wheels. It helps others to like you, listen to you, even buy from you. You don't buy things from people you dislike.

People will pay more to be entertained than to be educated.
– Unknown

Rules for using humor

1. **Targets**. Using humor is like handling a lethal weapon. It's important where you point it. The first target for humor is you. There's plenty of material here. Just ask your friends and the people you work with! Aiming the chuckle stick at yourself first is safe ground. Just don't work the territory so

much that we end up feeling sorry for you instead of laughing with you.

For example, when Johnny Carson hosted The Tonight Show, he would often start the show by tossing a pencil into the air and deliberately miss catching it and looking embarrassed. Following that, he poked fun at the dentures that caused him to lisp, his hair that was turning gray and his costly marital mistakes. After this successful self-deprecation, he slid to the second target of humor–institutions.

Institutions are the *non-changing structure* around us. On the Tonight Show the institution was the band and bandleader Doc Severinsen. Johnny routinely kidded Doc for his flamboyant clothing. Band members were also unmercifully targeted, questioned, and sarcastically impaled. For many humorists, the institution is the government, the IRS, the President of the United States, the Armed Forces, the postal system, the police, the court system, and their industry.

Lastly, for those skilled in walking on eggs, there is your audience. Here is where the land mines are waiting for the uninformed and careless comic wanderer. Without the mantle of certainty, I would leave this third target alone. Let the professional comedians go where angels fear to tread. Johnny only went to this area if he was having a successful show and the audience was participating. Sometimes he would accuse them of being "vicious" or "bloodthirsty." They didn't mind. In fact, they loved it, because he had already successfully covered humor's first two targets.

2. **Brevity** is humor's best friend. Less is often more. Avoid long stories. How long is too long? Test it out on friends beforehand and have them tell you. The longer a funny story is, the funnier it must be.

3. **Avoid trite sayings.** You must make jokes and humorous stories believable up to a point. Use factual, specific details that the audience can relate to; i.e., say "the Piggly Wiggly grocery" rather than "the grocery store." The more truthful

and specific the story sounds, the more your audience will get caught up in what you say.

4. **Profanity** is anything that offends others, even if it is fine with you. Know your audience and the situation. If there's any doubt, leave it out.

5. **Preparation.** Outside of extemporaneous levity, purposeful humor belongs to the prepared person. It's best to give it some thought beforehand and choose your best options. All those clever, off-the-cuff remarks that seasoned comedians make are often a result of years of practice. Occasionally, beginners who have had success with a few remarks make the mistake of thinking they can continue to be good with everything they say. Just remember, winning the lottery isn't a skill.

Ten humor tools

1. **Your mood.** The surest way to invite the lighter side into any talk is to shift into a playful mood. Likes attract. You don't have to change the agenda, but you do have to momentarily shift your perspective from rational to ridiculous. Some presenters I know can do this by telling themselves a favorite joke just before they are introduced, or reminding themselves of how they are when they speak to a baby or to their loved ones–relaxed, playful, fun.

2. **The detour**. In order to use this, you must first lead the listener away from the surprise at the end. First you establish a train of familiar thoughts in the listener's mind, and then you derail it. For example: "Most marketing letters used in business today have an opening, a body and a close encounter with the trash." Or "One department store's complaint policy is first: listen empathically; second: agree wholeheartedly, and third: offer to give all of your money back in New Guinea dimes." A slight pause between the second and third item lets the audience think ahead and guess what the next logical step would be. Interrupting their train of thought surprises them and creates humor.

3. **Opposites**. Here the words of an original statement are interpreted to create an opposite or alternative meaning. For example: "I know a guy that gets extremely nervous speaking to groups. Actually, when he speaks, he makes the whole audience nervous." Or "Outside of a dog, a book is man's best friend. Inside of a dog it's too dark to read." (Groucho Marx) Opposites are a ready technique for impromptu comments.

4. **Euphemism.** This is when you use an agreeable term to describe the disagreeable. For example: "He wasn't fired. He was granted an opportunity to explore a new career." Or "These dice are not loaded. They are merely prepared, the way you will be after this training."

5. **Callbacks**. The callback sounds like an impromptu thought, but it's really a calculated technique. Here's how it works: be alert to opportunities to repeat a phrase, name, place, or idea that got a chuckle the first time it was mentioned. Perhaps the person who spoke ahead of you said it, or the person that introduced you mentioned it. If the same audience found it funny the first time, whether it was something you said or someone else said, the mention of it again has a very good chance of rekindling a laugh. For example, if an earlier phrase like, "We'll just make up for the lack of profit margin by selling more volume…" got a rumble the first time, you could call it back a second or perhaps a third time (if it got a laugh the second time). Your saying the word "volume" as the solution to some other challenge could be one way to use it. The stronger the initial laugh, the longer you can milk it as a callback.

6. **Definitions**. Defining a normally serious subject from a comedic view is another starting point for humor. For example, you could take the word engineer and playfully define it as "Someone who is always right, but can't convince anyone." It helps if the target of the definition is you. In my case, "Did you know the definition of the French word *entrepre-*

neur actually means...unemployed?" Another variation of definition comedy is the top ten list. Just pose a question and fill in the ten most absurd answers you can think of, pretending that they were polled from the audience.

7. **Simile**. This common figure of speech can be used to create humorous comparisons. "That's rather like...blank, "or "That's as unlikely as ...blank." Example: "Going blank in the middle of a presentation is rather like being mule-kicked in the forehead and being expected to find your way back to the farmhouse."

8. **Logic transfer.** When you see defective logic in a situation, you can illustrate it humorously by transferring the same defective logic to another subject. Example: "Some speakers never consider an audience's attention span. They figure if you stay in your chair for all 146 slides, you must be enjoying yourself! I'm just glad these speakers didn't go into dentistry!"

9. **Skits**. Skits add needed variety; they're fun and they involve people. Think of a point you want to make and instead of explaining it yourself, form a committee of not-ready-for-prime-time volunteers to help you. Believe it or not, some people will jump at such an opportunity to share the spotlight, especially when they can feel protected behind the façade of a character. *Distinctions* can be effectively pointed out with skits. For instance, show the difference between the right and wrong way of doing a procedure; show the effect of before and after; competitor's services and yours; or the subtle differences of average and excellent. Skits instruct by showing opposites or the worst scenario.

   Even sophomorically done skits, performed with enthusiasm, are ten times more powerful than one more bullet point. Pick a point that you really want to get across to your listeners and ask yourself if it could be dramatized using a brief skit. Even the actors will get the point better since they are helping to teach it.

Where to find humor

1. Notice what makes you laugh, and better yet, write down what made the audience laugh in previous talks. You never know where humor will come from. The crucial thing is to somehow record it.
2. Know your audience. The more you know, the more opportunities you will find to play with them.
3. Self-examination. Look at your mistakes, pain and embarrassments. Example: I was in the audience for a half-day workshop where the lady facilitator announced a break, but forgot to turn off her cordless, lavaliere microphone before going to the ladies' lounge. Six hundred people couldn't help but hear her break over the PA system. When she returned, a girlfriend let her in on all the laughter. She immediately broke into a healthy laugh. Bloopers are even funnier when the actors break up laughing at their own mistakes. If you lay an egg and everyone knows, go with it.

Imagination was given to man to compensate him for what he is not; a sense of humor to console him for what he is.
– Francis Bacon

Useful humor

-   Captures or retains attention
-   Refreshes
-   Spurs creativity
-   Adds impact to the message. When the audience takes away a feeling, they take away the message with it.

Useless humor

-   Wastes time with irrelevant jokes

- Is allergic to editing, preparation, rehearsal or try-out
- Forces a joke on listeners, who are short on time
- Uses trite, worn-out phrases to try for a laugh. ("Rats leaving a sinking ship.") If you've heard it a thousand times already, they have too.

> *Wit is the salt of conversation, not the food.*
> – William Hazlitt

If you want to seriously persuade, then learn humor. Often, a strong statement spoken lightly will make more of an impression than one shouted. Watch the movie Mary Poppins again and learn from her. A pinch of laughter might be just what is needed to help listeners swallow what you're saying.

> *A little levity will save many a good thing from sinking.*
> – Samuel Butler

Additional insights

- The main reason people don't laugh is because they don't get it. An incomplete, vague or ambiguous message is usually the problem.
- Don't search high and low for the outlandish, and scorn the ordinary; you will touch more cords by finding what is funny in what you know to be true.
- If in doubt, throw it out. Using racial or ethnic slurs or talking about body fluids is always inappropriate. Even if the majority of the group would laugh, don't use it. In team-building, every link is important to the chain.
- To be fully spontaneous, you must be fully prepared.
- Criticizing someone less fortunate will boomerang. Human nature favors the underdog.
- Cartoons are almost always copyrighted. Create your own or

get permission from the artist.

- Humor is not written, it is rewritten. Learn to edit useless words. Strive for brevity.
- Humor is electric. Groups seated tightly together conduct it better.

EIGHTEEN

STORIES

Facts tell — stories sell.

Long before the age of technology, there were stories. Primitive man must have told stories as he stood between the fire and his enlarged shadow on the wall, reliving the day's hunt. With first-person conviction, he unfolded the scenes of the day's strategic survival to anyone willing to listen. As he informed and entertained, he demonstrated his competence as leader.

Today, we're still telling stories at the end of the day — the 6 p.m. news. Ordinary people who had no idea they would be on every major television station that night, tell the details of their news worthy experience to millions of interested viewers. Little has changed, because stories continue to serve both pre- senter and listener.

As the storyteller, you have the power to unfold and control a mental journey. You can lead the audience's focus down a path of discovery, where only you know the way and the destination. For the listener, stories provide a welcome distraction. Stories can relax audiences. They can allow us to escape our everyday challenges and problems and enter another world for a while. They can stir great emotions and passions that often lie buried in our day-to-day life.

An easier way to think

Good mental pictures get the job done. Our minds prefer to think in pictorial symbols. If I say the word "elephant," you probably see a large mammal with a long snout and floppy gray ears. What you don't see are the letters E-L-E-P-H-A-N-T. Though novels may consist entirely of words, we remember the stories they tell as a series of mental pictures. When these pictures move in an interesting or surprising way, we remember them vividly. Like movies, stories are rhetorical devices that can offer listeners a pleasant emotional experience. And when the story becomes real to them, they can cement our ideas into their minds.

Motivating and persuasive

Why do stories motivate others so well? They do the thinking for us. They make us feel. This ability to move listeners is a valuable tool for influencing others. They give our ideas impact, persuade, and make peers, customers and prospects pay attention. And when we're amused by life or caught up in emotion, we're more willing to change.

> *To rule the world — you must first amuse it.*
> –Oliver Seale

Personal stories and anecdotes

There are two types of stories, yours and someone else's. Your personal experiences are vital ingredients for your speaking toolbox. Somehow you must start a log of the one's you have already told, even if these were just a memorable experience you told a friend; write them down if they have potential to hold a larger audience's attention and make a point. Anecdotes, are someone else's experiences that when retold, help you make a point. Your own experiences are usually more powerful than the second type because when you tell something that has actually happened to you, you're surer of what you are saying instead of memorizing someone else's experiences and feelings. Another advantage is originality. No one can tell your first-hand incident as well as you. Even if someone tries, it will not have the same ring to it as you telling it. Remember: The singing group The Beatles, never got rich singing Buddy Holly songs. It wasn't until they record-ed their own song, *I Want To Hold Your Hand,* that things really started taking off for them. Told well, an original story becomes scarce, which creates value for the teller.

> *No man ever became great by imitation.*
> — Samuel Johnson

Anecdotes are also useful, but in a different way. They are usually shorter. They come with a point, so you don't have to formulate one, but you might find a way to make a different point using the same anecdote. For example: Asop's anecdote of the slow-moving tortoise and the self-assured hare, usually touts the lesson of the tortoise's perseverance and eventual victory, but the same story could also make a point about pride, or losing site of our goals, or completing a task. When re-telling an anecdotal story, resist the temptation to insert yourself into the scene as if it were an actual personal experience. It won't work for two reasons. People may have heard the anecdote before and second lying takes a toll on sincerity and believability. Just do your best to tell it simply and make your point.

Attaching the point to a story example

Stories don't always need a point, but if they're meant to do more than entertain, you'd better have one. Stating the point before or after the story is a matter of personal taste. Some people like to cite it before the story to telegraph the meaning they are trying to deliver. Others believe it works best to end with the point, after the story has captured attention, added drama, and built to an exciting conclusion. An argument can also be made for stating the point first and then again afterward for certain comprehension.

Let's say you wanted an anecdote that would mirror the point of "We all have a common goal." Here's how you might set it up by first making the point, second telling the story, and then reminding them again of the point in a slightly different way.

"You know, we all want to keep ahead of competition and minimize risk. Every one of us is looking for the same goal –to make this (company, project, team, etc.) successful. This common quest reminds me of the story of a man who phoned his friend one day. The phone he was calling only rang once, when a small voice on the other end said—

"Hello?"

"Hello! Billy?" the man said.

"Yes." said the boy softly.

"Is your Dad there?"

"Yes." he responded in a hushed tone.

"May I speak to him please?"

"He's busy." the boy said quietly.

"Okay. How about your mom? Can I speak with her?"

"She's busy." he said, again in a hushed tone.

"Alright. How about your big sister? Can I please talk with her?"

"She's busy too." he said softly.

Feeling rather agitated, the man said, "Billy! Can't anyone come to the phone besides you?"

"No." Billy replied.

"Well, why not?"

"Cause, they're busy. They're looking for me."

// Pause //

"I believe like you do, that we are all busy looking for ways to be more successful."

Look for opportunities to insert a story

Stories are most always more interesting than facts alone. Years ago, a female television interviewer who was interviewing swimming champion Mark Spitz held his hand up to the camera, saying: "Look, everyone. Look at this man's nails! They're longer than mine. How come, Mark?" As she let go of his wrist, Mark replied sheepishly, "I guess I just never broke the habit — the habit of growing them long when I was an Olympic swimmer. You see, four of my seven gold medals were won within hundredths of a second over the East German's best time. My nails were the first part of my body to cross the finish line." Here's the same information presented in bullet point fashion.

- Mark Spitz won seven gold medals in swimming.
- Fingernails – 1½ " long.
- Four medals were won by margins of hundredths of a second.
- Fingernails are the first part of a swimmer's body to cross the finish line.

Which method is more interesting? Which captures the audience's viewpoint for a moment? Which dramatizes the point? Which adds welcome variety to an everyday presentation?

Ken Bradford

How to tell a good story

1. In using a personal example, *don't be too general.* Start by picking an incident, a specific event. Provide the elements of when, where, who, why, how and what. These ingredients paint the mental pictures you need.
2. Make sure you choose an incident that *you found interesting.* If you want an enthusiastic response, be enthusiastic about your subject.
3. *Use descriptive details.* Skillful speakers seek words that paint the clearest pictures. Ministers who have never been to hell can tell you in detail what it feels like. For example, instead of saying "I walked into a store…" try "Yesterday, I strolled into the Stage Deli near my office on 45th Street…"
4. *Using spoken dialogue* will also perk up some ears. Inquiring minds pay attention to dialogue. People really do want to know what others are saying.
5. *Keep it short.* Many a good story has been spoiled by excessive length. The fewer words it takes to paint the picture, the better.
6. *What's the point?* Listeners will feel like their time has been wasted if you don't make a clear, relevant point. For added emphasis, use the bookend method: make the point before the story, tell the story, and then make the point again using slightly different words.
7. *Include contrast.* Remember the stories like Jack and the Beanstalk? The Tortoise and the Hare? Little Red Riding Hood? Classic stories. All make great use of contrast: patience versus speed, perseverance versus arrogant strength, and the power of innocence versus the power of evil. Contrast is easy. Just use the old tools of before and after, big versus small. A good time to get serious is right after a laugh. Consider these other pairings: predictability followed by surprise; underdogs and heroes; anger and joy; cheap versus expensive. Contrast gets the listener's attention. There's a good reason that the universal symbol for drama is two very different masks.

8. ***Move the characters.*** Movement means change and action, and action is what people want. Don't let the players in your story remain stationary for long. Make something happen to them physically, mentally or emotionally. During an interview, director George Lucas of Star Wars fame was asked how he edited the film. He replied, "It was easy. I just looked at each scene and cut out everything that wasn't exciting."

9. Don't discount your ***personal*** stories. Mine your own life experiences before using a canned saga — especially if they reveal your human frailties and strengths. Audiences will relate to the story and to you. Obviously, you don't want to share anything that would embarrass you and distract from the point. Lessons learned the hard way are great topics. Many times, if you can express your pain, you will find your power.

10. ***Have big gestures.*** Get your body and emotions into it. You're talking to an audience, not just one person. Your moves should expand to accommodate the size of the audience. Look at how a theater screen must be big to accommodate an audience. Be animated. When audiences see movement, they remember more and are more emotional about what they remember.

11. ***Rehearse.*** Find someone willing to provide an objective opinion. Avoid bouncing it off family members who may be positive, but blind to quality. Remember: If it doesn't work in practice time, it won't work in prime time.

People are likely to forget everything you say except for the pictures you paint in your stories. Story power is the ability to provide these memorable pictures. Try using it next time to explain an important message or complicated concept. Give your listeners a break — a mental break. Tell them a short, colorful, story with a point.

Ken Bradford

They say I tell a great many stories. I reckon I do; but I have learned from long experience that people are more easily influenced through the medium of a broad and humorous illustration than in any other way.
– Abraham Lincoln

Additional insights

- If is often easier to reflect on our own situation if we listen to a similar situation lived by someone else.
- Stories make facts come to life. Long after the presentation is over, the life-like images you paint is what's remembered.
- Don't condescend and tell the audience what they "should" know. A well-told story with a relevant point will suffice. You cannot teach a person anything; you can only help him find it for himself.
- If you use stories to entertain, look for the goofy and funny stuff that has happened to you. The audience wants to hear the crazy things life has dealt you and how you handled it.
- Using stories shows you have digested the topic enough to explain it simply. Many private moments of truth, can be powerful basis for stories.
- Learning to tell a good story takes practice. Record yourself to expedite the process.
- Repeat a key word occasionally to help dramatize your message.
- Relive the story, don't just relate it. Get into yourself so your voice, gestures, and tone will be in the present tense, connected and alive!
- People love good stories. Give them what they want and they will declare you a champion.
- One good painting may be worth a 1,000 words, but one good story can sell 1,000 paintings.

NINETEEN
PERSUASION

If you want to persuade, you must do more than inform.

The crowd watches breathlessly as a highly skilled archer draws his bow and takes aim. Everyone in the audience can see the target, but the archer sees only the bull's-eye.

What's your bulls-eye when it comes to speaking? Persuasion.

Think about it: the real purpose of a meeting is rarely just to give people information. Often, the primary goal is to persuade people to take action, change their thinking, stay on top of things, or improve behavior. In order to persuade your audience, you must first know what you are really after. Do you want them to give blood, buy land, achieve zero defects on the production line, or sign up for volunteer work?

A director of nurses held a meeting for a staff of over 100 RNs and orderlies. She spoke for more than an hour about the features of the hospital's new burn unit. Following her presentation, she complained bitterly because no one had signed up for a tour of the facility. She had given the crowd a lot of good information on the unit, but she hadn't given them any reason to take a tour, nor had she proposed one. She had aimed at the target but missed her bull's-eye.

Even knowledge of the truth will not necessarily
give us the ability to persuade.

At another event, a financial advisor assembled a panel of four professional money managers to speak at a public investment meeting. These were heavy hitters in the industry; each managed minimum individual portfolios of at least $250,000. The turnout was terrific. Over 200 potential clients attended the first of two public meetings. Each expert on the panel discussed investments for about 45 minutes. But, much to the disappointment of the meeting planner, only a handful of potential investors stayed afterwards and expressed an interest in becoming clients. Plenty of information had been covered, but no one had asked for action. Before the second meeting, the meeting planner refocused on his purpose. His obvious but unexpressed goal was to convert guests into clients. This time, he asked each speaker to mention a variety of specific ways that people could become involved with their firms. For example, prospects could request a portfolio review; subscribe to a newsletter; pose a written, confidential question; request a performance report on an investment; try a 30-day trial offer; arrange an appointment; or be included in an upcoming investor conference call. As a result, over the next two weeks following the second conference, 27 new guests became clients. Their combined investments totaled over $11,000,000.

Again, the lesson is: *know* what you want and *ask* for it.

Time is rarely the biggest problem.

An account rep for a software firm was preparing a sales presentation for senior managers of a large telephone equipment provider. His company provided him with 72 slides to describe the 16 service agreements they offered. At first he believed his biggest problem was lack of time. How could he possibly tell the managers everything in a 30-minute presentation?

After some thought, he decided that his real goal was not to expound on the company history and its sixteen service agreements. The bull's-eye was to have the managers see his company as a source for solving problems so they would buy his services. What the rep really needed to develop was a presentation that explained how his firm could meet the managers' needs. But he wasn't able to obtain their necessary information ahead of time, so he made his own list of possible issues and discussed these early in the presentation. Then he watched and listened for audience feedback. Based upon their reaction, he explained how his company provided solutions to each problem. As a result, the next time the telephone company encountered a problem, his firm was hired to solve it.

Keep in mind, the better you understand what you want and why you want it, the better your chances will be of acquiring It.
– Fred Jandt, *Win–Win Negotiating*

Twenty proven tools of persuasion

1. **Third-party testimonials.** Satisfied customers tell the best stories. Your audience will doubt your objectivity when you offer an opinion, especially when the way you will profit from your listeners' agreement is apparent to them. However, when one of your customers, whose situation was similar to your listeners', describes what you did to help — everyone

will listen. This third-party endorsement will help persuade your audience. Consider distributing copies of it on the endorsing company's letterhead. Make color copies of the original and use the same stationary as the original. Remember all your endorsements should reinforce your points and lead listeners toward the action you have in mind. After collecting several letters, you will want to sort them by industry or by buying motive, so you can have targeted evidence readily available.

2. **First-person, eyewitness stories.** There's a reason why the state governor owns a helicopter and flies into a disaster area to see a crisis firsthand. That information gives him specific evidence to use when he asks for federal relief funds. Get out from behind your desk and be the reporter. Go get the story. Other things being equal, the person with an eyewitness report will rarely if ever be at the mercy of someone with a mere opinion.

3. **Convert a key statement into a key question.** Change one of your best persuasive statements into a question. Instead of *telling* it — *ask* it, then pause. Which of the following phrases is stronger?

   (Statement) "If you knew you could not fail, you would make bigger plans."
   (Question) "What would your plans be — if you knew you could not fail?"

   (Statement) "We help business people conquer their fear of public speaking."
   (Question) "What could conquering the fear of public speaking mean to your career?"

Questions engage thought and begin the process of taking action. An added pause after a question allows time to let it sink into the listener's mind better, like letting a fishing lure float for a moment on the surface of the water before moving it, or like the way a comedian pauses after delivering a punch line.

A mediocre salesperson tells. A good salesperson explains. A superior salesperson demonstrates. A great salesperson inspires people to see the benefits as their own.
– Anonymous

4. **Create a brief survey first.** Surveys allow the other person to feel as if the ideas you present are their own. You don't need to know everything about your audience. What you really need to know if you want to persuade them, is:
   a) What problems do they have now that your proposal could help solve?
   b) What are their goals?
   c) What motivates them to make changes?
   d) What is the benefit to them if they take the action you suggest?
   e) Why are they considering a change now?

If you survey the audience first, you can avoid starting out with "Now I would like to tell you about our company, our products, and show you some of their features." Instead, you've earned the right to say, "Based on what we know about your business, there's a good possibility a few of our products would sell quickly to the customers in your market, generating a nice profit margin for you. Let's see if some of the items I would like to discuss with you today could be a fit with your merchandising initiatives."

Ken Bradford

Show how much you care by how much you remember about their concerns. Attention to other people's concerns is what distinguishes you as a leader. Note: You'll be likely to hear the most up-to-date issues by showing up early for meetings.

5. **Show what you're talking about.** As I've said all along, a list of six bullet points is rarely the best way to visually persuade an audience. If you already have twenty-five (unless it is a technical presentation that requires showing integral parts and pieces) or more slides, forget about using another one! Give everyone and yourself a break. Go get a physical example that relates to your presentation.

   A risk manager with a local airline company hired me to help her make a presentation to their insurance carrier. Her goal was to reduce the amount of money the company paid for covering the safety of airline passengers. Each of the past four years, she had presented statistical charts to show her company's safety record in the best light. Despite an enviable record, their premiums had risen for the past four years. She calculated the total number of lift-offs and landings the company's planes had made since beginning service in 1970 to be around 26,000,000 — an impressive number, but hard to appreciate out of context.

   Stopping by a coin dealer's store, she purchased a half-dozen pennies minted in 1937. When the day came to present her facts again, she brought out the pennies and gave one to each member of the insurance board, saying, "As you look at these pennies, I'm sure you noticed they were minted in 1937. I am using them to point out an interesting correlation between their age and our safety record. If you added up every minute of their existence since 1937, you would arrive at a number. This is the same number of times we have successfully lifted off and landed without a fatality. We are proud of this accomplishment and we feel justified in asking for a 10% reduction in our insurance rates this coming year." They got the point, and she got the reduction.

6. **Ask the audience to get involved.** Remember that one of the greatest needs of human beings is to feel accepted. Take a cue from Oprah Winfrey. Instead of presenting a one-hour monologue, she has conversations with the audience as she covers a central issue. She rarely criticizes their opinions, because she knows that would stifle involvement.

    Use Oprah's method and encourage your audience's involvement. The Socratic method is tried and true! Ask open questions like "What's your opinion?" then honor the answers.

    Ford Motor Company still asks, "Have you driven...." (you know the rest) because it works. Retail clothing clerks are trained to ask, "Would you like to try it on?" Get the audience involved, and you are on the right track to persuading them.

We are usually convinced more easily by reasons we have found ourselves than by those which have occurred to others.
– Blaise Pascal, *Pensées*

7. **Expand your gestures** to reflect the size of your ideas. If you're talking about "thousands," don't use two-cent gestures. A little drama entertains as it sells. For practice, try giving at least half of your gestures above the height of your shoulders. You'll be sure to make a better impression. For occasional emphasis, after a huge gesture, freeze for a two-count. After gesturing, if you bring your arms down so fast that they flop against your sides like a penguin's wings, you're going too fast.

8. **Understatement.** An understatement is composed of two sentences. The first is what you or your product *can't* do, which gets the audience's attention because it is negative. The second sentence is what you *can* do — which comes

across as more acceptable because the mind has just agreed to and accepted the first sentence. Example: "This package of Equal Sweetener won't change your life, but it will make it a little sweeter." Or, "This Volvo cannot go from zero to 90 MPH in six seconds, but — it can carry a family of six 400 miles on one tank of gas … safely."

9. **Use analogies.** People like associating something new with something they already understand. Analogies come easily if, after a key word, you add "like" or "as if," then finish the sentence.

In an earlier life I worked in the insurance industry while teaching public speaking at night. One day a friend of mine, Phil, called and asked if I would present him with a life insurance quote for one million-dollars. His bank had asked him to purchase one as collateral for a loan they were about to grant him so he could remodel his bowling center. Rushing over to his office, I handed him a computer printout of a proposed policy that showed the premium schedule and corresponding cash values. He thanked me and suggested I check back with him in three days. When I did, he informed me that he had decided to purchase a competitor's policy.

Rather than pout over the loss of a sale, I asked him if I could come by and learn something by looking at the other guy's proposal. He consented, and I drove over to look at it. I saw that the other life insurance agent had presented two proposals, giving Phil a choice (involvement and variety). Even so, price, coverage, and cost were almost identical to my proposal. My plan and the other two were within pennies of each other.

I was struck by two hand-made drawings the agent had inserted at the top of each of his proposals. The first one was a rectangle with a diagonal line crossing from the bottom left to the top right corner. The second proposal also had a rectangle but with a bold "X" connecting all four corners. I asked Phil, "Which one did you buy?" and he pointed to the one with the X and said, "That one, of course."

I knew Phil was a bowler. I knew he owned two bowling centers. I knew he always wore a ring and a necklace with the number "300" encrusted in chunky gold. I knew it took 12 strikes (X) to bowl a perfect game and he had done it twice. What I didn't know was the power of analogies.

Offer a comparison to something familiar to your audience. For most people, the best and sometimes the only way to "get it" is to "see it."

To compare is to understand – French Proverb

10. **Begin with sincere praise.** Think of the reason(s) it is an *honor* for you to be presenting. If it sounds at all trite, throw it out. Replace worn-out phrases like, "It's an honor to speak to you today, *because you're all so busy,*" or "*...because your time is so important.*" Instead, reveal an original sincere observation. Recall the opening remarks of Mary Kay Ash that I've already quoted. (Chapter 10: Involvement.) If she hadn't sincerely conveyed the sense that she had room in her heart for everyone present, she wouldn't have received fourteen minutes of applause. However, if you really can't think of a sincere reason why it is an honor for you to address a particular group, don't try faking it.

11. **Speak inclusively.** Inclusive language is: *"we," "all of us," "as many of you are already aware,"* or, *"as you can see," "as Bill or Susan pointed out earlier"* — instead of exclusive phrases such as: *"I always" "you should,"* or *"let me show you."* A decent guideline is to use ten "you's" for every "I." The presenter who is stuck using exclusive language, brimming with "I's," can quickly create an indifferent or even hostile audience.

12. **Raise your enthusiasm.** Some people call this passion or fire in the belly. Whatever it's called doesn't matter so long as you have it (and enthusiastic behavior is unmistakable). You've got to be fired up about something if you expect others to be. *If you speak with sincere emotion, the gods will grant you a second voice!*

13. **Talk first about others' interests.** Every audience listens better when you talk about their interests. Put another way, the other person is 10,000 times more interested in himself than he is in you and your concerns.

14. **Incorporate presentation formulas.** Persuasion isn't a clever closing technique. It is often a confident manner of using a formula. Formulas are guides for organizing your ideas so they flow to a logical, action-oriented conclusion. Here is a proven one:
    - *Summarize* the situation, by presenting an overview of the listener's past or current scenario.
    - Show *what's needed* to remedy, turn around or improve the situation.
    - Explain how the idea works. What are the *steps or ingredients* of the possible solution?
    - Reinforce the *key* benefits.
    - *Close* with a call for *action.*

One person's magic is just another's system. – Anonymous

An insurance agent, whom he had known for many years, once asked Henry Ford why he never got any of Ford's business. Ford replied, "You never asked me." As the saying goes, "If you don't ask, you won't get."

15. **Mention reasons for buying your idea *now*.** Create at least three reasons why your listeners should take action now. If

you can't think of three reasons why they should buy your idea now, think how hard it might be for the listener to think of three reasons!

"People will buy anything that's one to a customer."
– Sinclair Lewis

16. **Know your message cold.** Schoolteachers have topics to teach. Leaders have messages to share. There's a difference. You want to know your story cold and be able to boil it down and express it quickly if need be. You must see it simply and clearly in your mind before anyone else can grasp its true meaning. Once you really understand your core message, it's easier to organize all your points around it so they complement and accentuate its importance.

17. **Dramatize your ideas.** Opposites attract and help persuade because they grab our attention and convince. If you have an idea to explain and you want to punch up its value, try depicting the opposite. For example, a statement like, "You wouldn't invite the Queen over for lunch and serve peanut butter sandwiches, would you?" could be used to promote quality or raise standards. "Doc, I can't afford the surgery, could you just touch-up the x-rays?" might help dramatize the insignificance of price when the value is obvious. "What would you rather have, one hour with someone like Michael Jordan showing your team how to do a lay-up, or a week with a high school coach?" is a good way to explain the difference between paying for expertise versus paying by the hour. Contrasting statements make benefits easier to grasp. Politicians use them often. One of the most famous was Kennedy's "Ask not what your country can do for you…" The use of contrast made the rest of the statement so emphatic that virtually no one who heard it has forgotten.

18. **Repeat your key messages.** Repetition is crucial to reten-
    tion. Half an hour after a presentation, the average listener
    has already forgotten 40% of what was said. By the end of
    the week, that number has climbed to 90%. The more you
    repeat and illustrate your message, the more retention you
    can expect. A little repetition improves retention of your key
    message. Familiarity is soothing to the mind.

    Remember, too, that an audience can only remember at
    most three key points, so make those crucial points several
    times and in several different ways. But take caution not to
    erode those points with slide-heavy presentations.

19. **Use showmanship.** Make your product, services, or ideas
    stand out! Think about how other creative types are using a
    little showmanship to make the common become uncommon.
    About four years ago, I was making a connecting flight at the
    Atlanta airport. The terminal was crowded with travelers
    shuffling between gates and exits, but above the loud noise of
    mobile humanity came the piercing sound of click, click,
    click and POP! It was coming from the corner of the termi-
    nal behind a wall of people. I had to see for myself what was
    drawing the crowd. It turned out to be simply a man shining
    shoes, but he did it with much flair — popping the towel as
    he admired the glow he'd created and clicking two wooden-
    handled brushes together between strokes. It really was a
    show. Anyone who stopped to watch got a lesson in show-
    manship and persuasion from him.

20. **Politely persist.** Don't always try to accomplish everything
    in one meeting. Races don't always go to the swift, but to
    those who stay balanced and focused on their goals, creating
    little advantages every day. Coca-Cola sold just 400 cokes in
    its first year.

Fearless and Persuasive Speaking

Did you ever hear anyone say, "Gee, I love being *sold*"? Probably not. All of us guard the right to make our own decisions. People like to feel they're in control, that they have options and that they can reach their own conclusions. A persuasive presentation allows this to happen.

Will these 20-plus ideas guarantee persuasion? No. But they will provide you with an extra edge — and that is what this book is about. With a little extra preparation and the courage to try something different, you will distinguish yourself not only as a persuasive presenter, but also as a leader.

If you can speak to groups you can get by, but if you can skillfully communicate, you can work miracles.
— Jim Rohn

Additional insights

- See marketing presentations as a process, especially if they are not successful. Wait a week or even a month. Let your prospects know you are not still trying to change their decision, then return and sincerely ask how you could improve in the future. There will be another time when they will buy. Your extra interest could keep you among the top candidates for their business the next time around.
- Likeability is always a part of the buying decision. One of the best ways to be liked is to show a sincere interest in your audience.
- Consider taking an acting class. A little drama delivered at the appropriate moment can usually convince better than a barge-load of facts.
- Make the initial buying decision easy. Start by asking for a favorable decision on a very minor point. Once a person says, "Yes," there is a tendency to agree with what follows.
- Research listeners' motivations. Decide which inducement is best: moving toward a positive goal or moving away from

something negative. Your facts and features may be consistent, but your benefits should be tailored to your listener's motivations.

- Always provide a clear alternative to what you are arguing against. It's not enough to convince people to be against something. Make your alternative solution clear and attainable.
- Ask for outside feedback. An objective viewpoint can help eliminate defeating ingredients such as unclear benefits, condescending language, weak examples, barrier-producing body language and shop talk (inside terms that the listeners don't understand and therefore fear).

TWENTY

TACT

It's not everyone's style, but it never goes out of style.

When I was just beginning my career as a trainer, I had a class member named Ralph who had a special talent for not winning friends and *not* positively influencing people. He took pride in saying exactly what was on his mind. Even if you were on your deathbed you could still count on him to tell you, with complete honesty, how pathetic you looked.

Initially, class members found his frankness amusing, but as the term progressed everyone began to resent him, including me! I needed to talk to someone about my feelings, so one day I cornered a senior instructor. To my surprise, commenting on Ralph's lack of tact, he said, "You know, he's probably not such a bad guy. Maybe he just doesn't get it (diplomacy)."

I found this profound. He had reminded me that tact was something learned, not something inherited.

If you can display tact while under pressure talking to groups, you'll naturally be better at persuading and leading others. So how does one speak tactfully?

Five tools of tact

1. **Respect:** The most important factor. Watch the effect your words are having. While speaking, respect other people's ideas, differences, and feelings. If they accept what you're saying, they may smile, nod, or make direct eye contact with you. It they don't like it or are indifferent, they may frown, raise their eyebrows, shake their heads, or look away while pulling the corner of their mouths to one side. If these things are happening, you don't need a better audience; you need a better way of saying things.

2. **A gentler approach.** Always consider how your words sound to others. Once while buying shirts at Nordstrom's, I mistakenly picked out one that was not my size. As I approached the checkout counter, the saleslady discovered my error and said, "I'll be glad to go get the right size for you in the same color. I'll be right back." Notice that she didn't attribute blame for the error, opening the door to questions about who would have to go make the switch, or complaints about having to leave her post. She could of said, "I'll have to go get the right size" but she didn't. She had tact.

    With groups it might be the difference between saying, "I am not sure, but I'll be glad to find out and get back to you with an answer this afternoon..." versus "I'll have to look that up for you." The latter may sound OK if you're talking to yourself, but it costs nothing to improve it for the audience. Another example: " We don't have time to discuss that right now." versus " Could we discuss that at another time? So we can give it the time it deserves."

3. **Tone of voice**. Using tact also implies that you realize the effect that your tone of voice can have on others. A few years ago, two city workmen were digging up the street just a few feet from my driveway. In order to back my car out, I would need to cut the wheels sharply to avoid their work as my car entered the street. Before backing up I walked over to ditch they were working in and said rather softly, "I am going to be backing out now, okay?" They smiled and even offered to guide me as I slowly steered the car into the street. The very same words spoken in a more assertive, declarative manner with a neutral look on my face (see Chapter 6: Countenance) could have been taken differently.

   Psychologists believe that many audience members still harbor resentment for anyone who stands right over them and talks at length in a declarative voice. This can remind them of school years where authority figures — "big people" — towered over them all day. If you sense that you're lording over people, soften your voice and take a step back.

4. **Patience: A gift to ourselves.** The old Chinese proverb is true: "If you are patient in one moment of anger, you will escape a hundred days of sorrow." When you find yourself in a tense situation, instead of spouting a quick, fear-driven response, try offering a gracious one instead. To give yourself time to practice patience, try some "time-out" phrases like: "I think I know what you mean;" "You could be right;" "Okay. Who has another opinion?" "How do you mean?" It's been said that President Harry Truman was challenged one day as he was entering an airport. An obviously confused individual walked up to him, pointed a finger in Harry's face and said, "You're not Harry Truman! You're an imposter!" Without breaking stride, Harry replied, "You could be right."

5. **Direction: People reach up for class, not down.** Audiences are composed of individuals who are striving to maintain and

improve their social, economic, and intellectual levels. Your angle of approach should reflect your desire to confront them as equals or look up to them out of respect. To establish an equal plane you might say, "As many of you are probably aware..." instead of "Most of you probably don't know this, so I'll tell you..."

Talking down to the audience, or referring to peers or assistants in a disrespectful manner, is never acceptable. For example, "My girls can get that report to you this afternoon…" is talking down. Appropriate would be: "Our team can have it ready by this afternoon…" which is a level inflection.

To show respect and paint a higher vision you need to talk up to your audience. For example, "We all want the same outstanding results..." or "Based on the Herculean support you have already given..."

When people feel we are treating them on a level in keeping with their own view of themselves — or on a higher level — they are attracted to us and to our ideas.

Advice is not disliked because it is advice, but because so few people know how to give it. – Leigh Hunt

No one is born with tact, but as adults, we are responsible for learning how to cultivate it. How we communicate is a choice and by choosing the tools of tact, we can make the best possible impression on others.

Diplomacy builds organizations — and its absence can destroy them. Using tact will gain cooperation readily because it has a way of inducing others to express the best within them, and people who sense that they're at their best are ready for action.

Tact is sometimes hard to learn. Many successful managers, salespeople, and leaders acquired it through painful learning experiences. As Ben Franklin said, "Common knowledge is not always common action." Recently, someone who works with Ralph told me he's still likely to slap the Queen on the back and interrupt the Pope. It's just his style.

Tact is the art of making a point without making an enemy.
– Dr. Jim Olson.

Additional insights

(From *People Principles© 40 Reminders For Leaders*. Challenge yourself to apply these principles to your speaking style. *Even mediocrity applied is greater than latent genius.*)

- Before criticizing or complaining, consider silence as an option.
- First try to be understanding, and then try to be understood.
- Act. Don't react. Model values not moods.
- See more in a person than they see in themselves. Help others recognize their greatness.
- Be as enthusiastic about the success of others as you would be about your own.
- Assume responsibility for clear communications. Rather than say, "Do you understand me?" ask, "Am I saying this clearly?"
- Make absolutely sure the other person trusts you before offering constructive comments.
- Avoid saying, "I think you are wrong." Criticize the act, not the person.
- Persuade rather than coerce.
- There are times when forgetting can be just as important as remembering.
- Find the common ground as soon as possible.
- Treat everyone with respect, regardless of his or her position.
- Never give orders when you can ask.
- Your face radiates what is in your mind and heart. Smile.
- Consider the value of the relationship and the value of a single transaction.

Ken Bradford

- Give more understanding than advice.
- Confess your mistakes as soon as possible.
- Strive to become an excellent listener.
- Admit one of your own poor decisions before pointing out a similar error in another.
- Avoid petty arguments over petty issues.
- Correct in private, praise in public.

TWENTY-ONE

FACILITATING

Telling is not facilitating.

An audience that just listens is receiving a presentation. A group that must work together on initiatives needs the skills of a facilitator. The facilitator, like the conductor of an orchestra, achieves a common purpose by inspiring and harmonizing the audience's collective strengths.

Knowing how to skillfully facilitate groups is becoming increasingly important in the corporate world. As business models evolve, the traditional authoritarian, top-down management style is becoming more horizontal as managers and executives realize that two-way communication, worker empowerment, and a group approach are the most effective methods for motivating workers and leading change. Learning from Japan's quality- and productivity-team approaches, Americans are embracing the mathematics of good business: six people focused on the same idea are often smarter and more productive than one person going it alone.

Proper facilitation helps groups clarify their goals and process information toward a desired outcome. The art of facilitation demands mastery in maintaining subtle communication control while guiding the group interaction that determines the meeting's content and dynamics. The skilled facilitator knows when to back off, when to intervene, and how to reconcile different styles and viewpoints in order to become a catalyst for creative contributions.

When to facilitate and when to present?

Consider facilitating when your goal is:

1. Solving a problem
2. Planning group or department objectives, processes, revisions, restructuring
3. Improving production, quality, efficiency, customer service, morale
4. Coordinating systems, teams, tasks, departments, services
5. Creating a range of ideas to design an accountability or measurement system
6. Controlling spending, budgets, and processes
7. Raising awareness of an issue

The facilitator's essential tools

1. Excellent communication skills
2. Leadership principles
3. Flow management skills
4. Awareness of traps to avoid
5. A proven problem-solving formula
6. Questions to encourage team buy-in

Excellent communication skills

As a facilitator you must:

1. Be a complete communicator with both individuals and groups.
2. Be a superb listener. To the greatest extent possible, a skilled leader is aware of what group members are feeling and thinking even when they are not speaking. Scan the room for non-verbal gestures, especially body shifts and changes in facial expression.
3. Create dialogues, not monologues. Facilitators don't dominate, impose their own opinions, discourage participants or judge the value of their contributions. (Certain tools essential to the public speaker are of no use here.)
4. Be open. Facilitators must be honest, respectful, compassionate and willing to listen. They may challenge, probe, and question, but the intent is to enable the audience to explore and understand issues, ideas, and feelings.
5. Keep focused on both the process and the immediate tasks. A good facilitator provides a road map for the audience to process concepts and ideas in order to reach a certain conclusion.
6. Stay neutral. This requires a wide-open mindset, because the specific outcome is open.
7. Clarify and question to help members better understand what they are trying to create. Do this through direct questioning of a member or the entire group. At other times, you can try restating a thought or asking other group members to clarify what they have heard or said. For example, "Eddie, can you tell us a little more about what you mean by that?" or "Does anyone else have an example of what Jamie has pointed out?"
8. Be patient. Wait. If there is a lull, count to five before interrupting. Listen to the person speaking and observe body language to judge the mood of the group.

Ken Bradford

Leadership principles for meetings

In order for me to look good, everybody
around me has to look good. – Doris Drury, Chairman,
Federal Reserve Bank, Kansas City.

1. Have a clear purpose for the meeting. Your time is valuable and so is the participants'.
2. Follow the agenda.
3. Keep the meeting moving forward — tactfully. (See Chapter 20: Tact.)
4. Show respect for all ideas. Let participants know you value input by listening well and capturing their ideas on paper or a marker board.
5. When brainstorming, your initial goal is *quantity* of ideas. Help the group feel comfortable in offering their ideas, but avoid long debates and long discussions. (Keep the focus on attacking the problem, not attacking one another!)
6. Positively acknowledge contributors. Encourage more participation with your eye contact, nods, and smiles.
7. Try to get input from everyone in the group. Draw out any shy participants or late arrivers. People are more likely to support what they help create.
8. Spend less time talking about the *problem*. Spend more time working on the *possible solution* and the plan to achieve it.
9. Don't dominate the meeting.
10. Share authority and responsibility. Allow several people to be a part of the implementation plan. Keep a record of who is responsible for what.
11. Start and stop on time. For every minute you delay or go over your time limit, you can subtract two minutes spent building team morale.

Punctuality is disappointing if no one is there to appreciate it.
– Anonymous

Managing the flow

Never tell people how to do things. Tell them what to do and
they will surprise you with their ingenuity.
–General George Patton

Are you truly allowing others to provide content, or do you have your own agenda? The effective facilitator provides the structure and process; the audience provides the content (or the what). For example, a list of programming errors is the content; using brainstorming as a method for generating this list is the process. The facilitator guides the process. Keep the big picture in mind as you focus on the process rather than just the content of a discussion.

Determine what items you want to cover ahead of time. Circulate the purpose of the meeting and the agenda in advance to members and let them know what is expected of them. This preplanning allows people to bring necessary documents to the meeting and encourages them to think about the agenda beforehand.

Traps to avoid:

1. Seeing the facilitator's role as no more than leading a discussion.
2. Believing that facilitation is no more than asking questions of a group and soliciting their responses.
3. Being too structured — blind to alternate routes to the desired outcome.
4. Not having a guiding structure or a plan with estimated time frames.
5. Skipping from topic to topic. (You should have a plan for returning or rescheduling adjacent items for discussion.)
6. Not setting the right atmosphere or not acknowledging an obviously distracting circumstance.
7. Not staying focused on the present.

8. Unconsciously judging input by giving personal opinion to content.
9. Having more chairs than there are participants. Empty seats say, "I wonder why these people didn't want to come?" A full house says, "This is an important meeting and we're a unit."
10. Having too many people in a group. Group size will depend on the purpose of the meeting, but four to six people per group is recommended for green-light creative sessions. A large group might be a negative force if individuals feel hesitant to address a crowd.
11. Excluding the value of diverse opinions from different sources inside/outside the department or company.

It's not enough to be busy.
The question is: What are we busy about?
– Henry David Thoreau

A proven problem-solving formula

1. Introduce the situation.
2. State the situation as a one-sentence problem. Be clear about what aspect of the situation you will begin to solve.
3. Identify all possible causes of the problem. Resist the urge to stop collecting ideas after hearing the first five or six responses. Creative solutions are often reached after the more obvious or knee-jerk answers are elicited.
4. Identify several possible solutions to the problem.
5. Decide on the best possible solution. This could be an evolution from complementary solutions, but the initial direction or first step forward needs to be clear. Where will you begin? What will you do first?
6. Create a detailed plan of action. Don't expect the home office staff to take over, supply it yourself. People who are closest to the action are most qualified to establish a solution or plan.

Be specific and name names; pick dates, times, meeting locations. Avoid generalities like somebody, everyone, immediately, from now on, everywhere. These go nowhere! You can't plan a vacation with such generalities, and you can't make a business plan either.

WHO will take action?
WHAT exactly is to be done?
HOW will we do it?
WHERE and **WHEN** will the action be taken?

7.   Create a system to measure progress. Here again, the home office will not fly in and wrap this up for you. Unless it is obvious, you must usually figure this one out on your own. It is difficult to manage what we don't measure.

The secret to success is constancy to purpose.
– Benjamin Disraeli

Gaining buy-in

Buy-in requires you to stimulate thought response, but use minimal coaxing. Groups that have experience working together may only need a signal like, "Let's get started!" to begin. Newer, less-acquainted or less-trusting groups may need a little more direction like, "Let's begin. Which topic would you like to start with?" If necessary, you might begin with an assignment that leads them into an activity, such as, "This morning we're going to look at our average ticket size and how to increase it. I would like to begin by asking each of you to take out a piece of paper and list two ideas for …" If necessary, be prepared with structured exercises where you can provide feedback.

Be evenhanded. Make and maintain your connection with the group by building success one participant at a time. Visit with as many as possible before the meeting. Avoid judging. Assume that there is value in everyone's input.

It's important to realize that a continuum does exist and that it would be a mistake to develop a single structure for facilitating. Just as a nine-iron in golf cannot handle every situation presented on the course, neither can any specific meeting format handle all situations that arise.

The facilitator's role is a far cry from the speaker's. It requires in-depth knowledge of process, group dynamics, human relations, objectivity, and timing. By learning to fill it we can greatly increase our value to company and clients.

Take a leadership tip from Napoleon. After his stunning defeat of the Italians, he was asked how he made the French army cross the Alps in the dead of winter. He replied, "One does not make the French army cross the Alps. One leads it across." Seek facilitation opportunities to demonstrate your skills as a leader.

Additional insights

- The ultimate responsibility for staying on track and on time belongs to the leader.
- Spend more time on possible solutions and detailed plans than on interesting, but unproductive, aspects of the problem.
- Distribute meeting notes while memories are fresh. This will increase the likelihood of the follow-up action being taken.
- Have a ready supply of booster statements for the group, like: "Terrific!" "Good job!" "Tell us more!" "This is great!" "You guys (women) know how to get things done!"
- Consider doing without tables and arranging chairs in one large circle or several smaller circles, whichever would be more appropriate, thus eliminating back rows and onlookers.

TWENTY-TWO

VOICE

Distinct, but not totally defining.

Good news: you don't need to worry much about the sound of
your voice unless every time you answer the telephone, the
person on the other end says, "Could I please speak to your
mom?" What you say and who you are, is much more important
than how you sound. People may smile at your voice when they
first hear you, but it will not obscure your message in the end. As
you've learned, the most important way to overcome your fears,
connect with your listeners, and persuade them to buy your message is to have a conversation with them and speak as sincerely
as you would to an old friend. A jewel in a pig's nose does not
create beauty. Neither does a trained voice define personality and
character.

Ken Bradford

In law, what plea so tainted and corrupt
But, being seasoned with a gracious voice,
Obscures the show of evil?
– Sydney J. Harris

Students are often extremely self-conscious about the way they look and sound while giving their presentation. You've probably already been shocked when you heard your voice on tape for the first time. Watching yourself on videotape can be doubly alarming. In fact, people often tell me that having to watch themselves on video is pure torture. There is something fatal about critiquing yourself on tape and not being able to correct the flaws immediately.

Because of this, I avoid using recording equipment during initial sessions with beginning students. When you're just beginning, you need courage much more than technical training. The confidence to speak comes from focusing on communicating a worthy message, not from being too self-focused on how you sound.

The fear and insecurity many people have about speaking is more obvious in their voice than in any other aspect of their demeanor. If you're at war with yourself because you're insecure about your voice, the audience may quickly decide that you're uncomfortable with your message and that their first positive impression of you was wrong.

But with the right attitude about your voice and the use of some simple exercises to eliminate tension, you can gain more control of the physical apparatus that controls your speech. Instead of a potential enemy, you'll be able to consider your voice an ally. Invest a little effort preparing your voice ahead of time, and it will come through for you when the spotlight is on you, helping you deliver your message with power and conviction. Below are some practical tips for protecting and enhancing voice effectiveness:

Try humming. For a quick and excellent warm-up, hum a tune as loudly as you can. One opera singer I know carries a large balloon in his pocket and sings his warm-up exercises into it until it is near bursting. (After the air is released, he repeats the exercise as many times as necessary.) He finds that humming while inflating the balloon works just as well as singing into it. While the extra vocal strength doesn't last long, it will be enough to get you started speaking with excellent carrying power. It's easier to *maintain* the right "position" or "feel" for your voice than it is to find it, especially under pressure. Whispering is helpful, too, and not merely to spare a sore voice.

Prepare your voice in private. If you do resort to exercises, drugs, mints, "blasts" of breath-freshener, etc., you should do so out of sight of your audience. Not only are these preparations distracting and irritating, but they can hurt your credibility before the audience is assembled.

Don't talk too much, even at moderate volume, before your presentation. It will wear out your voice, especially if you don't drink plenty of water as part of your daily routine. *"Give every man thy ear, but few thy voice."* – William Shakespeare

Limit your consumption of dairy products a day or two before presenting. They create mucus, which causes you to clear your throat more often.

Try not to sleep with your mouth open. Easier said than done, but worth looking into. The vocal cords dry out when dehumidified air passes continuously over them.

If nasal passages are clogged, try using a humidifier to open up sinuses. If that's unsuccessful, see an ear, nose and throat doctor to find out if you have blocked passages.

Ken Bradford

Avoid even mild dehydration. Few of us drink enough water on a daily basis, and the throat is one of the first places to exhibit the affects of body dehydration. Air passing along the vocal cords dries the already water depleted tissue and causes dry mouth and throat. Extra perspiring accelerates the condition. Prepare for major speaking engagements by drinking extra amounts of water for two to three days prior to the event. You may also want to keep a glass of water near you while speaking.

> *A loud voice cannot compete with a clear voice,*
> *even if it's a whisper.* – Barry Neil Kaufman

Use singing exercises. Voices like being used in singing, as long as the demands aren't excessive or beyond their capabilities. Make time to sing. Auditioning for the church choir or singing at weddings may not be your goal, but the same exercises used to strengthen the singing voice can work wonders for the speaking voice. Don't strain, just use your natural vocal range. (There are cases of people losing their voices temporarily by trying to imitate someone they heard on the radio — and singing outside their normal register, i.e., a bass trying to imitate a tenor.)

Here are three simple exercises used by professional singers.

1. *Up-Down Glide Technique.* Say the sound "ah" and slide up the musical scale for two notes and then down two notes. This is especially good for expanding a monotone or a narrow speaking range. Graphically, it looks like this:

```
        Ah
   Ah       Ah
   Ah       Ah
```

   Don't strain. Practice doing this comfortably for two minutes a day.

2. Ka-Ga-Ha. Say Ka-Ga-Ha in succession for seven times. Remember to open up your lips and the back of your throat. This exaggerated exercise is great for improving articulation. Again, don't strain. Try to relax as you exercise your muscles.

3. My friend the opera singer developed some interesting ways to prepare his voice. One method he developed is called "gulping. " To try it, place your hand over your mouth and pinch your nose shut between your thumb and forefinger, then hum with your mouth and nose completely closed off. You'll notice that you can't make a sound without lowering your larynx. Actively lowering your larynx to force air through it creates a gulping sound, and making your voice "work" in this way will have the rather amazing effect of increasing your vocal strength and endurance. When you use your voice after humming or gulping in this way, you'll be surprised at the volume and "ring" you have picked up without having spoken a single word.

The thing that influenced me the most was the way Tommy Dorsey played his trombone. It was my idea to make my voice work in the same way as a trombone or violin –not sounding like them, but "playing" the voice like those instrumentalists.
– Frank Sinatra

You may find some or all of these exercises helpful, or you may find that they offer you little or no improvement. Just remember, in the last analysis, your desire to be heard by everyone in the room is the best guarantee that you will be. If your message is important enough, and you have a genuine desire to communicate it, your natural vocal endowment and the instinctive way you make use of it will be sufficient.

Ken Bradford

Microphones. At some point, most people who speak frequently in public will have to speak into a microphone. Obviously, you should practice with any sound system before using it. Given that you have been able to familiarize yourself with the system, you should also know that microphones can exaggerate certain vocal handicaps. If your voice is hoarse or a little raucous on a given day, be careful to stay a little further from the mike than usual. Even if your voice amplifies well, you shouldn't use the microphone as a crutch — holding it with both hands, closing your eyes and in general acting as if it, instead of your audience, is the reason you're so excited. Hold it just slightly below your chin to avoid "popping" your words into the receiver. Using a microphone won't become a distraction if you are careful to maintain eye contact throughout your speech.

Use these tips if you need them before a presentation, but again, don't worry too much about your voice. Many great speakers don't possess a commanding voice, yet they are charismatic leaders nonetheless. Why do we love listening to them? I believe it's because their enthusiasm and excitement is contagious. When they speak, you feel what they feel. You feel that you've shared their experiences. You laugh at their funny stories. You choke a little at their sad ones. These speakers aren't afraid to express their emotions. They can take any dry topic and make it exciting, because they are excited, not just about the topic at hand, but about life.

Your approach to the moments becomes your life.

As you build upon your string of emotionally successful speaking opportunities, you will dare to release more feelings and excitement, creating a symphony of life through your voice. Strengthen your vocal signature, by resolving to speak with even more conviction, sincerity, urgency and sometimes fun. Show real enthusiasm and heart to any audience, and they'll find it irresistible.

Fearless and Persuasive Speaking

Just because your voice reaches halfway around the world doesn't mean you are wiser than when it reached only to the end of the bar. – Edward R. Murrow

Additional insights

- Try not to clear your throat excessively while in front of an audience.
- When there is loud applause prior to your speech, or any loud sound, take advantage of it to hum. You don't have to try to hum a tune, just hum on different speaking levels: high, low, or in between.
- Pay attention to the audience at all times to see if anyone is straining to hear you. It's up to you to judge how much volume will be necessary to reach all your listeners. Ask someone to sit in the back row and listen to you, before the audience arrives, so you will feel confident about your projection from the start.
- When you're practicing your speech, try raising your voice to emphasize certain points. Then see if some of these points could be made more effectively by lowering your voice and speaking with greater intensity.
- Rest your voice. Use pauses, especially before or after a major point. Stop occasionally to gauge your audience's reaction. Maintaining eye contact during pauses is the best assurance that your voice will never become droning and that your audience will want to hear the rest of what you have to say.
- Drinking alcohol the night before a presentation may harm your voice the next day, primarily because of dehydration. Celebrate any way you want *after* your presentation.
- The No. 1 way to improve your voice is to talk about a subject you are passionate about.

TWENTY-THREE

TEAM PRESENTATIONS

Team presentations don't have to be seamless, but it helps if they're united.

I s there really safety in numbers? Group presentations divide responsibility, but multiply risk. As a team member, you own a piece of the group's ultimate success or failure. Each of you must shape words and actions to accommodate the rest of the cast, so that collectively you will deliver a clear and persuasive message. In addition to winning the individual battle of nerves, your group must win the approval of some sort of judge. Like theatrical performers, your team is putting on a show and accepting the reviews — good or bad!

Necessary steps

-   Design a persuasive strategy.

- Gather superior information.
- Define roles.
- Choose the best techniques to deliver the message.
- Rehearse as a team.
- Critique and refine.

Designing a persuasive strategy

Brainstorm the situation as a group from all angles. First, put yourself in the audience's moccasins. What are their goals? How are they prioritized? What matters most to this client? What action do you want as a result of your presentation? How can you prove that your proposal is the best course of action? What must be gained? What must be avoided? What are the intangibles? Work as a group and capture the group's input on a flipchart or marker board so everyone can see the genesis of the strategy.

> *As a rule of thumb, involve everyone in everything.*
> – Tom Peters

Create a simple outline that leads toward a desired result. Example: Problem > Strategy > Solution. Everything must point logically to the end in mind.

Gathering information

Not only do you want factual information here (and not opinion), you want superior information. Superior information is:

- Gathered about as well as *from* the client. Maybe it comes from surveying the client, key employees, customers and suppliers, even competitors. The client's needs are *understood* — not *guessed at* — as much as possible.
- The most recent statistics, trend, demand, style, etc., accord-

ing to the best experts.
- Captures and documents your competitive edges.
- Succinctly and forcefully conveys your message.
- New to the client, though it has already been thoroughly challenged by you, by objective outsiders, supervisors and competitors.

Often, you must be the reporter and get what you need. No one will hand it to you. And while you're at it, make sure you research your competitors, too. Assess their strengths and vulnerabilities.

Defining roles

Who will play what part? As in a play, you need a script before you start casting. Again, form follows function. It is sometimes possible to cast before you have a script, but then you are asking your cast to adjust to it later. Perhaps they can, but with a known script you can make a better choice of presenters.

Pick a team leader. Circuses have ringmasters, ships have captains, and news teams have anchors; so pick someone as spokesperson. Audiences like having one person as director. You also need someone to coordinate and keep the group on track.

Decide who should be presenting. Who is necessary? Who could play which role best? Who would the audience want to see? Maybe they will want to see some of the key people who would implement the plan or service. Do they want to hear from the people who managed the last project or someone from the home office, or both? After you decide on your best strategy and roles, give a little more thought to casting. If the presentation is produced like a well-scripted, well-directed play; you need the best people to present it.

Ken Bradford

Choosing the best techniques to deliver your message

After the text is written, decide how you can maximize the impact of your information. (See Chapter 15 on Variety and Chapter 19: Persuasion.) Your delivery tools might include analogies, eyewitness stories of success or disaster, props, visual samples of important forms, third-party brag sheets, rhetorical questions, sage quotes, big names, large 24-inch x 30-inch colored photos to show offices or equipment, and summarized case studies.

Your competitors will probably show a number of slides to tell their story. If you use slides as well, judge each one critically. If you can make a point more effectively with a personal incident, demonstration, or testimonial letter, toss the slide and use the more dynamic method. Remember, your enemy is sameness.

Even when you are using variety by having several people lead the presentation, you still must guard against data dumping and bullet overload. Practice not being verbally driven by the slide sequence. For example, avoid the rut of saying, "This next slide shows us ..." or "Here we have..." Mix it up. Make a point without using a slide or make the point and then use a slide to complement what you just said.

Personalize the presentation without spending money. Spend your energy instead.
- Learn the names of some audience members and use them occasionally.
- Take a pre-program survey. Ask audience members questions about things like their values, goals, and opportunities for the future. Then get their individual permission to use these quotes in your presentation. Build one slide or flipchart page with their quotes on it. They will definitely pay attention to this one slide.
- Use a yellow highlighter pen and highlight an interesting point in each handout. Duplicate the highlighting for the

matching overhead transparency. This will help personalize the material to the audience.

- If the audience has a theme or motto, include the phrase into a relevant point of your presentation.

Rehearse as a team.

To look like a team, rehearse as a team. Seamlessness is a utopian goal. The main thing is to spend enough time to look organized. This means knowing your opening words, your messages, the transitions from presenter to presenter, and answers to important questions.

> *Either we're pulling together or we're pulling apart.*
> – Anonymous

Avoid the temptation to avoid rehearsing. Excuses like, "I'll be covering this and you cover that and we'll be great," or "I think I only need five minutes for my part — trust me…" can come back to haunt you later. You wouldn't wear rumpled clothes to work. A live rehearsal irons the wrinkles out of your presentation as surely as a hot iron smoothes out a cotton shirt.

Practice your opening statements. Your goal is to establish immediate rapport and make your audience want to listen. While most openers will do, an excellent one is well planned but looks natural. Depending on the situation, include some or all of the ingredients below:

1. A self-introduction
2. An attention-getting opener
3. An overview of the subject under consideration
4. A sincere and specific compliment. If you like the audience, nothing might be more important than your concise, sincere expression of this fact.

Time everyone's part. As you design and rehearse, fit the whole presentation to an allotted time. Practice until your team can finish a little early. Try to have a minute or two to spare should you need it to expand on a point. If you don't need the extra couple of minutes, the audience might be pleased with your efficiency, and your team will stand out as better organized that the ones that ran long.

Choreography. Whenever possible, pick out the area with the fewest phone lines, busy windows, stacked chairs, food, doorways or other distractions and use that as the front of the room. If you're on foreign soil, ask what the audience usually considers the front of the room. If there is no obvious stage area, you will have to create the area in your imagination. How well you can envision this will influence how well the audience is able to accept it too.

Ask the facilities person to set up the room as you need, but once you get there, work with what is there and don't complain. Even before the presentation starts, the audience and perhaps their staff are evaluating your cooperativeness.

Script the hand-offs. Like a relay race, practice how you will introduce the next presenter. Keep introductions light, brief and informative. If you rehearse this, the hand-offs will help demonstrate how your team works well together.

Plan the introductions. Ask team members how they want to be introduced, but be sure to include what is most relevant to the occasion. For example, if you divided the presentation into four parts that address the client's four main concerns, leave off lengthy accolades and introduce the next person as the best team member to address one of those concerns.

Never leave the stage bare. Hold the stage until the next presenter arrives at the front, then don't step in front or upstage him or her. Sit down immediately to avoid becoming a distraction to the audience or speaker.

Know your closing sentences well. The ending needs to incorporate your central message, but also needs to be said with a slight twist so that it doesn't sound too repetitive.

Anticipate common and challenging questions. Plan the Q & A. Ask your own questions and rehearse your best answers. Ask peers to challenge your facts. Develop superior information that has already been challenged by several objective people before presenting it to the real audience.

Critique and refine.

Remember what you're selling: trust. Your company's history and people's titles are important, but if they don't trust you — you're sunk. They won't believe you can perform as expected. You must build your credibility and narrow the gap between your team and the audience. Remember also that one of your goals is to prove value. Know and address issues your listeners value. Money in itself is worthless. We will gladly trade it for what we value.

> *How can I trust someone to manage a multi-million dollar project if he or she can't manage a half-hour speech?*
> – Bill Hewlett, Co-founder Hewlett-Packard

Here is a checklist to see if you're including what's important and eliminating what reduces your effectiveness.

Little killers

- Starting your presentation with the word "uh."
- Offering apologies like, "We're sorry that our chief designer couldn't be here today, because without him, it's difficult to explain how we work as a team…" or "We can't adequately

tell you everything in the time (you the client) allotted us..."

- Looking uninterested, not because you are — quite the opposite, but because you let fear over-ride your cheerful facial expression. See Chapter 6 on the importance of Countenance.
- Displaying second-class posture. Sit up. If standing, you don't have to imitate a Marine sergeant with your shoulders back and chest forward, or stand confrontationally with your arms crossed. Just stand tall and balance your weight. The audience can tell by looking at you if you are focused upon their needs or yours.
- Using fonts or visuals too small for audience members to read. When preparing visuals, make sure they are readable for the audience. If an eagle in the back row had to squint and lean forward, they're too small!
- Presenting visuals too complex to be fully understood. The rule is: it's okay to have some complex visuals if you can explain them simply. If you can't, simplify it.
- Being unfamiliar with a visual! Surprises are for wars and birthdays. Rehearse until you can easily communicate the meaning of all your visuals.
- Failing to turn off your cell-phone. Embarrassing, but forgivable. Of course you must never answer it during the presentation.
- Using two podiums on either side of the stage, with two speakers sharing information alternatively. It's not an original idea. Often speakers suggest it to halve the pressure, but from the audience, it plays like a slow tennis game with an imaginary ball. The back and forth movement is annoying. Often, it looks like neither one of you is competent enough to stand on his own.
- Exhibiting tactlessness with your own teammates. When you must correct a misquoted number or misleading statement cited by one of your teammates, do so with tact. Instead of saying, " You're wrong." try saying, "Rather" or "It's actually." or "Yes, but in this case, it's..." How you treat your own people when they are vulnerable tells the

audience how you will treat them once you have their money. (See Chapter 20: Tact.)

Distractions to avoid

Inappropriate dress. Nothing you wear should draw attention away from your message. Dress simply and traditionally. Watch out for large bracelets, flyaway hair, and buttons that are undone. If you're careless about your appearance, the audience may believe that you'll be careless with their concerns, too. So give yourself a once over — twice, using a full-length mirror.
If you can't find a mirror, ask a companion for a quick inspection. Is your tie tied or half-hitched with the shirt showing above it? Are your coat pockets "ready for take off" or halfway in? Fix them the way your tailor intended. Is part of your lunch scaling your tie? Look at your teeth. Is spinach a part of your smile? Are your shoes shined? Keep a quick-shine kit in the car.

Lack of attention. Nothing distracts an audience like an uninterested panelist who stares into space or keeps checking his watch. Even if you know every word of someone else's speech, stay glued or you'll distract people who are hearing it for the first time. Don't talk or wave to others while someone else is speaking. Even if you're bored, be an actor and pretend that you're not. If you have to convey something to a team member, use a notepad and slide it near them.

Busy human scenery. If you're not presenting, you're part of the scenery. Sit down. If there are enough chairs, take one. Having people up front to stand beside you may look like a show of strength, but it dilutes the speaker's message and makes the other members of the team look like they're in a hurry to leave.

Parasite props. Keeping agenda notes or a clipboard with you while speaking is okay so long as you don't play with them. But be careful: even a few dramatic gestures with notes in your hands will wave off your message, like a flagman on an aircraft carrier.

Put pens and markers down or you'll be tempted to use them like a swagger stick or continuously taking the cap off and on. No one likes being talked to while someone is shaking an object at them. It makes dogs cringe and humans raise their guard.

If you have a tendency to play with coins in your pockets; donate your small change to the waitress.

A good presentation won't guarantee a win,
but a bad one can cause a loss.
–Ken Bradford

Additional insights

- Keep the energy up. The entire program should have a good pace, but not feel rushed.
- Pay attention. Immerse yourself in your presentation. Stay extremely focused and interested in showing your desire to serve. If you don't seem enthusiastic NOW, why would the prospect believe you would feel more interested LATER?
- Speak to the entire group. Don't favor one side of the room. Make everyone feel included. They all have a vote.
- Communicate desire. If you feel passionate about the project, let it show. Sincere pride and enthusiasm attract!

Additional resources

The Leaders Course®

Since 1992, over 3000 individuals have strengthened their leadership abilities through The Leaders Course® in Effective Speaking and Human Relations. This book presents the real-life wisdom developed from thousands of hours of classroom experience.

The Leaders Course® is much more than a public speaking class: it is a powerful, proven system for self-empowerment. Through ample encouragement and personalized reinforcement from a veteran instructor, students acquire the practical life-skills that allow them to realize their own unique potential and distinguish themselves as true leaders. In mastering their fear of public speaking, class members discover an unexpected bonus, too: newfound confidence to make improvements to the way they interact with others and the challenges of everyday life.

Many students are amazed at how quickly they learn to organize their ideas, control their nervousness, and deliver a persuasive message to virtually any size group. The Leaders Course® is taught in a completely positive atmosphere, in which all class members have multiple opportunities to practice their skills in front of a live audience.

As the students encourage each other and track each other's progress every week, they also become more aware of their own communication style.

By the end of the course, an exciting transformation has occurred. Tension has been replaced by enthusiasm. Shyer personalities have blossomed and bolder personalities have discovered humility. Skills have been acquired that no one believed were possible.

The results speak for themselves. Thousands of Leaders Course® graduates now take delight in their newfound ability to remember names, think on their feet, and lead effective, results-oriented meetings. Many attest that the human relations principles and relationship-building skills they learned continue to help them throughout their lives – both personally and professionally.

Class size is limited to allow equal time for participation and feedback. Along with a copy of *Fearless and Persuasive Speaking*, students receive a desktop set of 40 Leadership Principles; Booklets on listening, remembering names, holding better meetings, and principles of teambuilding; a participants guide; class photo, framed diploma and 20 hours of classroom instruction.

The course is approved for continuing education credits by several trade and professional organizations.

For more information on The Leaders Course®, please visit our website at www.LeadersCourse.com or Email to: kenbrad@airmail.net

NEED MORE LEADERS?

10 Benefits of The Leaders Course® training

1. Overcome fear of speaking to groups
2. Learn to remember names, personalize communications and raise accountability
3. Acquire the skills of an "exceptional" good listener
4. Become efficient at using 40 proven leadership principles for gaining greater cooperation and reducing conflicts. Here are four of the principles for example:
   > Admit mistakes quickly
   > Take responsibility for clear communications
   > Never say "I'll try" just to please, when you really mean "No"
   > Praise in public and correct in private
5. Sell yourself and your ideas effectively
6. Know how to organize ideas and present them confidently in front of groups
7. Increase awareness of the unproductive power of criticizing and blaming
8. How to build trust, long-term relationships and repeat business
9. Make better use of time in meetings and achieve above-average participation
10. Expand and enhance business, personal, and civic horizons

Five habit-forming sessions. Once a week (half-day) for five weeks. A powerful opportunity to evaluate and improve present methods of communicating and dealing with people.

Common sense is not always common practice –Benjamin Franklin, 1772

Unique content is not the value of the course. Thousands of leadership courses offer the same subject matter. The Leaders Course® owes its success to its unique training methods taught in a non-threatening atmosphere, five-weeks of application outside of the classroom, weekly reporting to measure results, and the word-of-mouth advertising from satisfied graduates across the nation.

Participants must be willing to work hard, select meaningful personal goals, and be held accountable for applying the material. The goal of the course is habit-forming behavioral improvement, not note-taking and short-term awareness.

This is a limited enrollment class.

See the following page or visit **www.LeadersCourse.com** for more information about bringing the course to your area.

Have a *GROUP* that needs more Leadership Skills?

With as few as a dozen participants you can bring The Leaders Course® to your area.

Schedule an On-Site Class!

For organizations with 12 or more candidates, we offer training to integrate your business goals with classroom training objectives. On-site training where each week, the instructor does the traveling, not the students -- saves you time and lowers the per-person investment.

To discuss bringing this exciting program to your area call

The Leaders Course® office at: **972-814-5758** or Email kenbrad@airmail.net